Marketing Plans That Work

Marketing Plans That Work

Targeting Growth and Profitability

Malcolm H.B. McDonald
Warren J. Keegan

Butterworth–Heinemann
Boston Oxford Johannesburg Melbourne New Delhi Singapore

Library of Congress Cataloging-in-Publication Data

McDonald, Malcolm.
    Marketing plans that work: targeting growth and profitability /
Malcolm H. B. McDonald, Warren J. Keegan.
        p.   cm.
    Includes indexes.
    ISBN 0-7506-9828-4
    1. Marketing—Planning. I. Keegan, Warren J. II. Title.
HF5415.13.M3691832   1997
658.8'02—dc21   97-7401
                                                                      CIP

British Library Cataloguing-in-Publication Data
A catalogue record for this book is available from the British Library.

The publisher offers special discounts on bulk orders of this book.
For information, please contact:
Manager of Special Sales
Butterworth–Heinemann
313 Washington Street
Newton, MA 02158-1626
Tel: 617-928-2500
Fax: 617-928-2620

For information on all business publications available, contact our World Wide Web home page at: http://www.bh.com

10 9 8 7 6

Printed in the United States of America

Contents

1 Understanding the Marketing Process

In chapter 1, we discuss marketing concept, company capabilities, marketing environment, customer wants, marketing mix, confusion about what marketing is, what the customer really wants, whether consumer, service, and industrial marketing are different, and finally, whether you need a marketing department. Readers who are already familiar with the role of marketing in organizations may want to go straight to chapter 2, which begins to explain the marketing planning process.

THE MARKETING CONCEPT

In 1776, when Adam Smith said that consumption is the sole end and purpose of production, he was describing what in recent years has become known as the *marketing concept*. The central idea of marketing is to match the capabilities of a company with the needs and wants of customers to achieve a mutually beneficial relationship.

Marketing: match between capabilities and wants to achieve mutual objectives

It is important to understand the difference between the marketing concept and the marketing function, which is concerned with the management of the *marketing mix*. For the sake of simplicity, these are often written about and referred to as the four Ps: product, price, promotion, and place. We have added a fifth P, probe for marketing intelligence (information gathering and research). Management of the marketing mix involves using the various tools and techniques available to managers to implement the marketing concept. However, before any meaningful discussion can take place about how the marketing function should be managed, it is vital to understand the idea of marketing itself (the marketing concept), and it is this issue that we principally address in this chapter.

COMPANY CAPABILITIES

Marketing is a matching process between the capabilities of a company and the wants of customers. It is important to understand what we mean by the capabilities of a company. To explain this more fully, let us imagine that we have been laid off and have decided to set ourselves up in our own business.

The Role of Marketing in Business

What causes success in the long run, by which we mean a continuous growth in sales, earnings, and the market value of a company's shares, has been shown by research to depend on the following four elements:

1. A core product or service that customers value and the ability to adapt the product or service offered to changing market needs. Marketing has a major input into the process that produces products and services that customers value.
2. Excellent, world class, state-of-the-art operations. Marketing should, of course, have an input to defining operational efficiency in customer value terms.
3. A culture that encourages employees to be creative in ways that lead to constantly increasing customer value. Bored and boring people, for whom subservience and compliance are the norm, at best give average performance. Only people who are engaged and excited by what they are doing are capable of creating a sustainable competitive advantage.
4. A corporate culture that is not dominated (because of its history) by production, operations, or financial orientation. Evidence shows that marketing makes an essential contribution to the achievement of corporate objectives.

The role of marketing is to ensure (1) that the company focuses on the total environment of business, markets, competition, customers, government, and trends and (2) that it uses all knowledge and experience to develop a mutually beneficial relationship with its customers.

THE MARKETING ENVIRONMENT

The matching process, referred to earlier, takes place in the *marketing environment,* which is the milieu in which the firm is operating. The environment in which we operate is not controlled by us, and it is dynamic. It must be constantly monitored. An important constituent of the marketing environment is our competitors, for what they do vitally affects our own behavior as a company. Because what our competitors do so vitally affects our decisions, it is necessary to monitor them and other elements of the environment and to build this into our decision-making process. In chapter 10 we show how this can be done.

The *political, fiscal, economic,* and *legal* policies of the governments of the countries where we sell our goods and services also determine what we can do. *Technology* is constantly changing, and we can no longer assume that our current range of products will continue to be demanded by our customers. For example, the introduction of nondrip paint had a profound effect on what had traditionally been a stable market. People discovered that they could use paint without causing a mess, and eventually this product was demanded in new kinds of outlets. One can imagine what happened to paint manufacturers who continued to make only their traditional products and to distribute them only through traditional outlets. Such a change would also call for a change in pricing, promotion, and distribution policies. Failure to realize this and to act accordingly would probably result in commercial failure.

So far, we have talked about the three constituents of a matching process:

- The capabilities of a firm
- The wants of customers
- The marketing environment

CUSTOMER WANTS

Although we deal with this subject in chapter 3, let us briefly turn our attention to the subject of customer wants. Perhaps one of the greatest areas of misunderstanding in marketing concerns this question of customer wants. Companies are accused of manipulating innocent consumers by making them want things they do not really need. If this were so, the new product failure rate would not be as high as it is. The fact is that people have always had needs, such as home entertainment. What changes in the course of time is the way people satisfy these needs. For example, television is commercially viable because people have a need for information and entertainment, and television is a way of fulfilling that need.

What's the sense of producing anything inexpensively, efficiently, or perfectly if no one wants it?

All customer needs have many different ways of being satisfied, and whenever people have *choice* they choose the product that they perceive as offering the greatest benefits to them at whatever price they are prepared to pay. What this means, in effect, since all companies incur costs in taking goods or services to market, is that profit through customer satisfaction is the ultimate measure of the worth of what the commercial firm is doing. Low cost, efficiency, quality, or any other measure is not a criterion of effectiveness. There is little point in producing anything efficiently or perfectly if people do not want it. Research has shown that there is a direct link between long-run profitability and the ability of a firm to understand its customers' needs and provide value for them. In the not-for-profit sector, customer satisfaction is a proxy for profitability.

Any organization that continues to offer something for which there is a long-term fundamental decline in demand, unless it is prepared to change to be more in tune with what the market wants, will go out of business. Even less sensible would be for a government, or a parent company, to subsidize such an operation. We know that to go on producing what people do not want is economically wasteful and futile, especially when people can get what they want from abroad if they cannot buy it in their home country. Any company that lags behind its competitors in offering value to customers will lose its share of the market and eventually go out of business.

Central to the question of customer wants is an understanding of what we mean by a *market*. To start with, customers, not markets, buy products. A market is merely an aggregation of customers who share similar needs and wants. In reality, most markets consist of a number of submarkets, each of which is different. For example, the airline market consists of freight and passenger transport. The passenger side can be subdivided further into VFR (visiting friends and relatives), high rated (business travel), and charter. Failure to understand the needs of these very different customer groups would result in failure to provide the desired services at an acceptable price. The ability to identify groups of customer wants that we are able to satisfy profitably is central to marketing management.

THE MARKETING MIX

Managing the marketing mix involves the use of the tools and techniques of marketing. For the matching process to take place, we need *information*. The external and internal flow of marketing information (marketing research) and database management are discussed in chapter 10.

Having found out what customers want, we must develop products to satisfy those wants. This is known as *product management* and is discussed in chapter 4. We must charge a price for our products, and this is discussed in chapter 8. We must also get our products into customers' hands, giving time and place utility to our product. Distribution and customer service are discussed in chapter 9.

All that remains now is to tell our customers about our products, for we can be certain that customers will not beat a path to our door to buy whatever it is we are making. Here we must consider all forms of communication, especially advertising, personal selling, and sales promotion. These are discussed in chapters 6 and 7. Finally we must consider how to tie it all together in the form of a marketing plan. This is so important that the whole of chapter 2 is devoted to a discussion of the marketing planning process.

CONFUSION ABOUT MARKETING

It is a sad reflection on the state of marketing that in spite of more than seventy-five years of marketing education, ignorance still abounds concerning what marketing is. The marketing process and philosophy will never be effective in an organization whose history is one of technical, production, operations, or financial orientation. Such enterprises may
Veneer or have adopted the vocabulary of marketing and applied a veneer of mar-
substance? keting terminology, but they are not customer driven.

It is naive to assume that marketing is all about advertising. Advertising is only one aspect of communication. Many firms waste their advertising expenditure because they have not properly identified their target market.

Many companies spend more on advertising when times are good and less on advertising when times are bad. Cutting the advertising budget often is seen as an easy way to boost profits when a firm is below its budgeted level of profit. This tendency is encouraged by the fact that the budget can be cut without any apparent immediate adverse effect on sales. Unfortunately, this is just another classic misunderstanding about marketing and the role of advertising. A management that cuts the advertising budget in response to poor sales acts as if advertising is caused by sales. It is naive to assume that advertising effectiveness can be measured in terms of sales when it is only a part of the total marketing process.

The following are areas of confusion about marketing:

1. *Sales.* One chief executive officer aggressively announced to everyone at the beginning of a seminar, "There is no time for marketing in this company until sales improve!" Confusion between marketing and sales is still one of the biggest barriers to be overcome.

2. *Product Management.* The belief that all a company has to do to succeed is to produce a good product is still widespread. Sony's beta video cassette recorders, Apple's Macintosh computers, the Concorde, and the many thousands of brilliant products that have seen their owners or inventors go bankrupt prove the error of this belief.

3. *Advertising.* This is another popular misconception. The annals of business are replete with examples such as British Airways, which before hiring professional management won awards with brilliant advertising campaigns while failing to deliver the goods. Throwing advertising expenditure at the problem is a popular way of tackling deep-rooted marketing problems.

4. *Customer Service.* The "have a nice day" syndrome is having its heyday in many countries. The concept was popularized by Peters and Waterman in *In Search of Excellence.* Many organizations now know, of course, that training everyone to be nice to customers does not help if the basic offer is fundamentally wrong. For example, in the case of railway companies like Amtrak, although customers like to be treated nicely, they find it more important to get where they are going on time.

5. *Selling.* Selling is only one aspect of communication with customers. To say that it is the only thing that matters is to ignore the importance of product management, pricing, distribution, and other forms of communication in achieving profitable sales. Selling is the part of the process in which the transaction is actually clinched. It is the culmination of the marketing process, and success is possible only if all the other elements of the marketing mix have been properly managed. Imagine having a horse that did not have four legs. The more attention paid to finding out what customers want, to developing products to satisfy these wants, to pricing at a level consistent with the benefits offered, to gaining distribution, and to communicating effectively with the target market, the more likely we are to be able to exchange contracts through the personal selling process.

WHAT DOES THE CUSTOMER WANT?

We have to beware of what the words "finding out what the customer wants," which appear in most definitions of marketing, really mean. Customers do not really know what they want. All they really want is better ways of solving their problems, so one of the main tasks of marketing is to understand customers and their problems in depth so that we can continuously work on ways of making life easier for them.

ARE INDUSTRIAL, CONSUMER, AND SERVICE MARKETING DIFFERENT?

The central ideas of marketing are universal. It makes no difference whether we are marketing furnaces, insurance policies, or soft drinks.

Beyond Traditional Market Research

In 10 years of developing the minivan we never once got a
letter from a housewife asking us to invent one. To the skeptics,
that proved there was not a market out there.

—Hal Sperlich "Father of the Chrysler Minivan"

Do not merely satisfy your customers, amaze them!

(From Gary Hamel and C. K. Prahalad [1994], *Competing for the
Future.* Boston: Harvard Business School Press, p.101.)

Problems sometimes arise, however, when we try to implement marketing ideas in service companies and industrial goods companies. A service does not lend itself to being specified in the same way as a product because it does not have reproducible physical dimensions that can be measured. With the purchase of any service, there is a large element of trust on the part of the buyer, who can only be sure of the quality and performance of the service after it has been completed. The salesperson selling the service becomes part of the service, because the sales encounter is one of the principal ways in which the potential efficacy of the service can be assessed. A service product cannot be made in advance and stored for selling "off the shelf" at a later stage. Nonetheless, apart from differences in emphasis, the principles of marketing apply to services in exactly the same way they apply to physical products.

Industrial goods are goods sold to industrial businesses or institutional or government buyers for incorporation into their own products, to be resold, or to be used by them within their own business. Principal types of industrial goods are raw materials, components, capital goods and maintenance, repair, and operating goods and equipment.

Information about industrial markets is not as readily available as information about consumer goods markets, which makes it more difficult to measure changes in market share. There are other difficulties besides these that make marketing in the industrial area difficult.

Unfortunately, to solve this problem many companies recruit a "marketing person" and leave that person to get on with the job of marketing. Such a "solution" can never work, because the marketing concept if it is to work at all has to be understood and practiced by all executives in a firm, not the marketing manager alone. Otherwise all departments continue to behave as they did before, and the marketing person quickly becomes ineffective.

EVOLUTION OF THE MARKETING PHILOSOPHY

The consumer-oriented philosophy of business that emphasizes meeting consumer wants and needs is called the *marketing concept.* A good illustration of how this approach to marketing works is Honda's rise to prominence in the U.S. automobile market. Honda started by satisfying U.S. drivers' desire for fuel-efficient cars with the economical Civic in 1973. When consumers' preferences changed to roominess, comfort, and performance, Honda brought out the Accord, which became the best-selling car in the United States in the early 1990s. When consumers began to look for luxury in their cars, Honda introduced the Acura. Every change in Honda's product line was prompted by a changing consumer need. Every success came from offering value to customers.

Marketing philosophy has changed over the years. Figure 1-1 compares the old telling-and-selling approach with the new idea (1960) of focusing on the customer and with the contemporary philosophy of marketing as a way of doing business and relationship marketing. In the early days of marketing, marketers focused exclusively on selling. That approach was succeeded by the idea of managing the marketing mix—the four Ps presented at the beginning of the chapter. In the now or future concept of marketing, the marketing-mix approach has expanded to include all knowledge and experience. The aim of marketing is to create a mutually beneficial relationship with customers. The end result of mar-

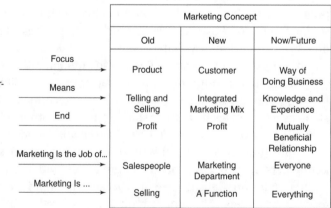

Figure 1-1
Marketing Is Everything
Source: © Warren Keegan Associates, Inc. Reprinted by permission.

	Marketing Concept		
	Old	New	Now/Future
Focus	Product	Customer	Way of Doing Business
Means	Telling and Selling	Integrated Marketing Mix	Knowledge and Experience
End	Profit	Profit	Mutually Beneficial Relationship
Marketing Is the Job of...	Salespeople	Marketing Department	Everyone
Marketing Is ...	Selling	A Function	Everything

keting is a relationship that means long-term growth and profitability for the company and maximum satisfaction for the customer. This now or future concept of marketing is also referred to as *relationship marketing.*

Relationship marketing is an approach to marketing in which a company endeavors to build continuing relationships with its customers that promote both the long-term growth of the company and the maximum satisfaction of the customer. Satisfying customers necessitates staying in touch with people's changing needs and ensuring the company's ability to fulfill those needs with new product lines and marketing strategies.

In cutting-edge marketing, the marketing concept has been extended to integrate concern for customer satisfaction into every corporate function. That is why you find discussions of relationship building in many chapters of this book. In chapter 2, for example, we explore how the concepts of quality (excellence in products and the ways in which they are produced) and relationship building are interrelated.

QUESTIONS SUCCESSFUL COMPANIES ASK

1. What is the *deep need* that we satisfy?
2. What do our customers really want?
3. How can we implement the now concept of marketing?
4. What should be the role of our marketing department?
5. Should we set marketing objectives based on last year's performance or on an assessment of the market and competition and our value proposition?

2 The Marketing Planning Process

In chapter 2, we discuss marketing planning, why it is essential, the difference between tactical and strategic marketing plans, the marketing planning process, marketing audits, why they are necessary, the form of the audit, the place of a marketing audit in a management audit, when an audit is performed and who performs it, the results of audits, the relation between marketing planning and corporate planning, assumptions, marketing objectives, marketing strategies and programs, use of marketing plans, budgets, the contents of a strategic plan, and mission statements.

WHAT IS MARKETING PLANNING?

Market planning: the planned application of marketing resources to achieve marketing objectives

The marketing plan is an outline of a design to accomplish an objective. The objective is to create value for customers at a profit, or in the now concept of marketing, a mutually beneficial relationship. The marketing plan ties together your assessment of market needs and wants, the strengths and weaknesses of your organization and those of your existing and expected competitors, and your design for creating value to satisfy the needs or wants of targeted customers at a profit. The marketing plan includes action plans (who is to do what when) and a vision, strategic intent, goals, and objectives.

This process can be defined as *marketing planning*, which is the application of marketing resources to achieve marketing objectives.

Marketing planning, then, is simply a logical sequence of activities leading to the setting of marketing objectives and the formulation of plans for achieving them. Companies generally go through a management process in developing marketing plans. In small, undiversified companies this process is usually informal. In large, diversified organizations the process is often systematized. This process is very simple in concept and involves a situation review, formulation of basic assumptions, setting objectives for what is being sold and to whom, deciding how the objectives are to be achieved, and scheduling and costing out the actions necessary for implementation.

Each plan is unique, but in almost all cases, a plan includes financial forecasts and budgets in detail for the first year and in outline summary for subsequent years. The first part of a marketing plan is the *situation analysis*. This section includes but is not limited to a strengths, weaknesses, opportunities, and threats (SWOT) analysis. The situation analysis is followed by the plan itself. The problem is that although the process is simple to understand, the practice is the most difficult of all marketing tasks. The reason is that it involves bringing together into one coherent plan all the elements of marketing. For this to happen, at least some institutionalized practice is necessary. It is this institutionalization that seems to cause a great deal of difficulty for companies.

The purpose of this chapter is to explain as simply as possible what marketing planning is and how the process works before the more important components of marketing planning are explained in later chapters.

One reason companies have difficulty developing marketing plans is that management has little guidance on how the process should be managed. That is, proceeding from reviews to objectives, strategies, programs, budgets and back again until a compromise is reached between what is desirable and what is practicable, given the constraints that every company has.

Another reason companies find it difficult to develop a marketing plan is that a planning system itself is little more than a structured approach to the process just described. Because of the varying size, complexity, character, and diversity of company operations, there can be no such thing as an "off the rack" system that can be implemented without fundamental amendments to suit the situation-specific requirements of each company. The degree to which any company can develop an integrated, coordinated, and consistent plan depends on an understanding of the marketing planning process itself as a means of sharpening the focus on all levels of management within an organization.

WHY IS MARKETING PLANNING ESSENTIAL?

There can be little doubt that marketing planning is essential when we consider the increasingly hostile and complex environment in which companies operate. Hundreds of external and internal factors interact in a bafflingly complex way to affect our ability to serve customers at a profit. Consider for a moment the four typical objectives that companies set—maximizing revenue, maximizing profits, maximizing return on investment, and minimizing costs. Each one of these has its own special appeal to different managers within the company, depending on the nature of their function. In reality, the best that can ever be achieved is a kind of "optimum compromise."

Apart from the need to cope with increasing turbulence, environmental complexity, intense competitive pressures, and the sheer speed of technological change, a marketing plan is useful for the following purposes:
- To help identify sources of competitive advantage
- To force an organized approach

- To develop specificity
- To ensure consistent relationships
- To inform
- To obtain resources
- To receive support
- To gain commitment
- To set objectives and strategies

Strategic or tactical? What's the difference?

ARE WE TALKING ABOUT A TACTICAL OR A STRATEGIC MARKETING PLAN?

Our research has shown that in the murky depths of organizational behavior in relation to marketing planning, confusion reigns supreme, nowhere more so than over the terminology of marketing. Few practicing marketers understand the importance of a *strategic* marketing plan as opposed to a *tactical* or operational marketing plan.

The problem is simple. Most managers prefer to sell the products they find easiest to sell to customers who offer the least line of resistance. By developing short-term, tactical marketing plans first and extrapolating them, managers succeed only in extrapolating their own shortcomings.

It is a bit like steering from the wake—all right in calm, clear waters, but not so sensible in busy and choppy waters. Preoccupation with preparing a detailed one-year plan first is typical of many companies that confuse sales forecasting and budgeting with strategic marketing planning—in our experience the most common mistake of all. This brings us to the starting point in marketing planning—an understanding of the difference between *strategy* and *tactics*.

Strategy describes the direction a business will pursue and guides the allocation of resources and effort. Put another way, *strategy* describes the business we are in and the business we are becoming. It also provides the logic that integrates the perspectives of functional departments and operating units and points them all in the same direction. The strategy statement for a business unit is composed of the following three elements:

- A business definition that specifies the area in which the business will compete
- A strategic thrust that describes where competitive advantage is to be gained
- Supportive functional strategies

Tactics are short-term actions taken to achieve the implementation of a broader strategy. *Marketing strategy* is a statement of how a brand or product line will achieve its objectives. The strategy provides decisions and direction regarding variables such as segmentation of the market, identification of the target market, positioning, marketing mix elements, and expenditures.

Figure 2-1 shows the old style of company in which little attention is paid to strategy by any level of management. In this company, lower levels of management are not involved at all, whereas senior management and the board spend most of their time on operational and tactical issues.

Figure 2-2 is a representation of companies that recognize the importance of strategy and manage to involve all levels of management in strategy formulation.

The rules are as follows:

- Develop the *strategic* marketing plan first. This entails emphasis on scanning the external environment and early identification of forces emanating from it and development of appropriate strategic responses that involve all levels of management in the process.
- A strategic plan should cover five years. Only when the plan has been developed and agreed upon should the one-year operational marketing plan be developed. Never write the one-year plan first and extrapolate it.

The emphasis throughout this book is on preparation of a strategic marketing plan. The format for an operational or tactical plan is exactly the same, except for the amount of detail. It is discussed in chapter 12.

Figure 2-1
Tactically Oriented Company

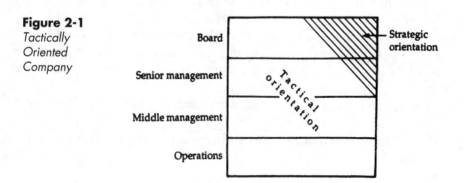

Figure 2-2
*Strategically
Oriented
Company*

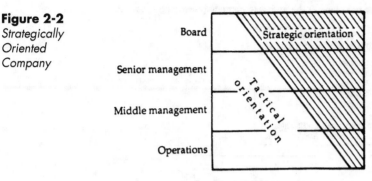

THE MARKETING PLANNING PROCESS

Figure 2-3 illustrates the stages in the development of a marketing plan.
A strategic marketing plan should contain the following:

- A mission statement
- A financial summary of the revenue, expenses, cash flow, and earnings to be achieved during the planning period
- A summary of the principal external factors that affected the company's marketing performance during the previous year together with a statement of the company's strengths and weaknesses in relation to the competition. This is called a SWOT (strengths, weaknesses, opportunities, threats) analysis.
- A list of assumptions about the key determinants of marketing success and failure
- Overall marketing objectives and strategies
- Strategies to create the resources needed to implement value creating programs for customers
- Marketing programs containing details of timing, responsibilities, and costs with sales forecasts and budgets

Each of the stages is discussed in detail later in this chapter.
The dotted lines in Figure 2-3 indicate the reality of the planning process, in that it is likely that each of these steps will have to be taken more than once before final programs can be written.
Although research has shown these marketing planning steps to be universally applicable, the degree to which each of the separate steps in the diagram has to be formalized depends to a large extent on the size and nature of the company. For example, an *undiversified* company generally uses less formalized procedures, because top management tends to have

Figure 2-3
Stages to Arriving at a Marketing Plan

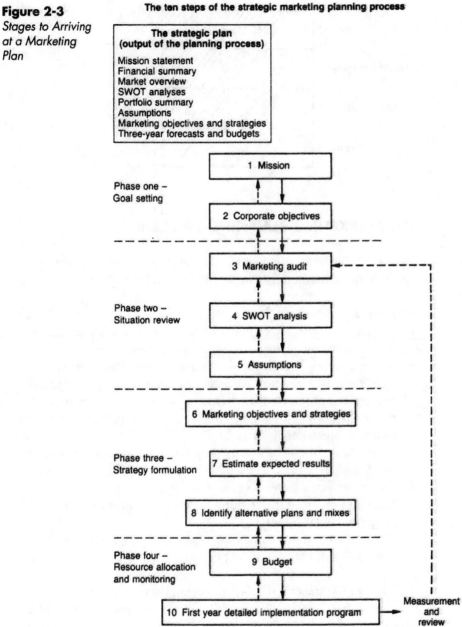

The ten steps of the strategic marketing planning process

The strategic plan (output of the planning process)
Mission statement
Financial summary
Market overview
SWOT analyses
Portfolio summary
Assumptions
Marketing objectives and strategies
Three-year forecasts and budgets

Phase one –
Goal setting

1 Mission

2 Corporate objectives

Phase two –
Situation review

3 Marketing audit

4 SWOT analysis

5 Assumptions

Phase three –
Strategy formulation

6 Marketing objectives and strategies

7 Estimate expected results

8 Identify alternative plans and mixes

Phase four –
Resource allocation
and monitoring

9 Budget

10 First year detailed implementation program

Measurement
and
review

A Swedish company selling batteries internationally tried unsuccessfully three times to introduce a marketing planning system. Each effort failed because of a lack of commitment by top management to the planning process. Without a commitment, those charged with introducing the planning found that there was great resistance to planning on the part of local managers. Without the commitment of top management, the local managers resisted, and planning efforts failed. The director of planning was replaced three times in this company. A commitment to planning by top management, training of managers, and careful thought about resource requirements would have largely overcome this company's planning problems.

greater functional knowledge and expertise than subordinates and because the lack of diversity of operations enables direct control to be exercised over most of the key determinants of success. Situation reviews, setting of marketing objectives, and other tasks are not always made explicit in writing, although these steps still have to be taken.

In contrast, in a *diversified* company, it is usually not possible for top management to have greater functional knowledge and expertise than subordinate management. The whole planning process tends to be formalized to provide consistent discipline for those who have to make the decisions throughout the organization. Either way, a substantial body of evidence shows that formalized marketing planning procedures generally result in greater profitability and stability in the long term and help to reduce friction and operational difficulties within organizations.

When marketing planning has failed, it has generally been because companies have placed too much emphasis on the procedures themselves and the resulting paperwork, rather than on generating information useful to and consumable by management. When companies delegate marketing planning to someone called a "planner," the plan invariably fails, because planning for line management cannot be delegated to a third party. The real role of the planner should be to help those responsible for implementation to formulate a plan. Failure to recognize this simple fact can be disastrous.

The audit answers "Where is the company now?"

THE MARKETING AUDIT

A *marketing audit* is a formal, systematic review of the executed marketing strategy and plan. It may take the form of an external audit by independent experts or an internal audit by members of the marketing organization. An audit examines records and procedures and identifies problems in the environment, within the organization, and between the organization and its suppliers. The goal is to see how well the firm is applying the marketing concepts—creating value for its customers at a profit. The marketing audit enables management to look beyond routine sales reports and market share estimates. Managers can use an audit to question the productivity of the marketing dollars.

Why Is an Audit Needed?

Often the need for an audit does not manifest itself until things start to go wrong for a company—declining sales, falling margins, lost market share, underutilized production capacity. At times like these, management often attempts to treat the wrong symptoms. Introducing new products or dropping products, reorganizing the sales force, reducing prices, and cutting costs are just some of the actions that are taken. Such measures, however, are unlikely to be effective if more fundamental problems are not identified. Of course, if the company can survive long enough, it might eventually solve its problems through a process of elimination. Problems have to be properly defined, and the audit is a means of helping to define them.

To summarize, the audit is a structured approach to the collection and analysis of information and data in the complex business environment and an essential prerequisite to problem solving.

The Form of the Audit

Audits can be external or internal.

Any company performing an audit is faced with two kinds of variables. First are variables over which the company has no direct control. These usually take the form of what can be described as *environmental, market,* and *competitive variables.* Second are variables over which the company has complete control. These we can call *operational variables.* This gives us a clue as to how we can structure an audit; that is, in two parts—an external audit and an internal audit.

The *external audit* is concerned with the uncontrollable variables, and the *internal audit* is concerned with the controllable variables. The external audit starts with an examination of information on the general economy and then moves on to the outlook for the health and growth of the markets served by the company. The purpose of the internal audit is to assess the resources of the organization as they relate to the environment and the resources of competitors.

The Place of the Marketing Audit
in the Management Audit

The term *management audit* merely means a company-wide audit that includes an assessment of all internal resources against the external environment. In practice, the best way to perform a management audit is to conduct a separate audit of each major management function. Thus the marketing audit is merely part of the larger management audit in the same way that the production audit is.

Table 2-1 is a checklist of areas to be investigated as part of the marketing audit.

TABLE 2-1   Marketing Audit Checklist

External audit	Internal audit
Business and economic environment	*Marketing operational variables*
Economic	Own company
Political/fiscal/legal	Sales (total, by geographical location, by
Social/cultural	industrial type, by customer, by product)
Technological	Market shares
Intra-company	Profit margins/costs
	Marketing procedures
The market	Marketing organization
Total market, size, growth and trends	Marketing information/research
(value/volume)	Marketing mix variables as follows:
Market characteristics, developments and	Product management
trends	Price
Products	Distribution
Prices	Promotion
Physical distribution	
Channels	
Customers/consumers	
Communication	
Industry practices	
Competition	
Major competitors	
Size	
Market shares/coverage	
Market standing/reputation	
Production capabilities	
Distribution policies	
Marketing methods	
Extent of diversification	
Personnel issues	
International links	
Profitability	
Key strengths and weaknesses	

The marketing audit should not be a last-ditch attempt to define a company's marketing problem.

Each of these headings should be examined with a view to isolating factors considered critical to the company's performance. The auditor's first task is to screen an enormous amount of information and data for validity and relevance. Some data and information will have to be reorganized into a more easily usable form. Judgment is needed to decide what additional data and information are necessary for definition of the problem.

The auditing process has the following two basic phases:

1. Identification, measurement, collection, and analysis of all facts and opinions that affect a company's problems
2. The application of judgment to uncertain areas that remain after the initial analysis

When Should a Marketing Audit Be Conducted?

A mistaken belief held by many people is that the marketing audit is a last-ditch, end-of-the-road attempt to define a company's marketing problem, or at best something done by an independent body from time to time to ensure that a company is on the right track. Because marketing is such a complex function, we believe it is essential to perform a thorough situation analysis at least once a year at the beginning of the planning cycle.

Successful companies, besides using normal information and control procedures and marketing research throughout the year, start their planning cycle each year with a formal review, through an audit-type process, of all factors that have had an important influence on marketing activities.

Who Should Conduct the Marketing Audit?

A critical issue in conducting a marketing audit is who should do it. Should the audit be conducted by a company's own executives and managers or by outside consultants? We believe that periodically it is wise to engage outside consultants to perform a marketing audit. Every company is at risk of becoming blinded to reality by the influence of company culture. This is especially true for companies who have great products, or even worse, insanely great products. No amount of internal auditing will break through a company or organizational "superiority complex," which may be causing the company to miss the mark in terms of understanding what customers want and need.

Few if any outside consultants, however, have the in-depth knowledge of markets, customers, company culture, and the industry that company line managers have. This is an argument for an audit conducted by the company's line managers in their areas of responsibility. Objections to this type of audit center on the problems of lack of time and lack of objectivity.

In practice, the problems are overcome by institutionalization of procedures in as much detail as possible so that all managers have to conform to a disciplined approach and by thorough training in the use of the procedures. Rigorous discipline must be applied from the highest down to the lowest levels of management involved in the audit. Such discipline is usually successful in helping managers avoid the sort of tunnel vision that often results from lack of critical appraisal.

What Happens to the Results of the Audit?

The only remaining question is what happens to the results of the audit? Some companies consume valuable resources conducting audits that bring little by way of actionable results. Indeed, there is always the danger that at the audit stage, insufficient attention is paid to the need to concentrate on analysis that determines which trends and developments will actually affect the company. A checklist ensures the completeness of logic and analysis, but the people conducting the audit must discipline themselves to omit from their audits all information not central to the company's marketing problems and opportunities.

It is essential to concentrate on analysis that determines which trends and developments will actually affect the company. Because the objective of the audit is to determine the marketing objectives and strategies of a company, it follows that it would be helpful if a format could be found for organizing the findings.

One useful way of organizing findings is in the form of a SWOT analysis. This is a summary of the audit under the headings internal strengths and weaknesses as they relate to external opportunities and threats. Detailed guidance on how to complete a SWOT analysis is contained in chapters 3, 4, and 12.

A SWOT analysis contains no more than four or five pages of commentary that focuses on *key factors* only. It highlights internal *differential* strengths and weaknesses in relation to competitors' *key* external opportunities and threats. A summary of reasons for good or bad performance is included. The analysis is interesting to read, contains concise statements, includes only relevant and important data, and emphasizes creative analysis.

To summarize, conducting a regular and thorough marketing audit in a structured manner goes a long way toward giving a company a knowledge of the business, trends in the market, and where value is added by competitors; the audit is the basis for setting objectives and strategies.

HOW MARKETING PLANNING RELATES TO CORPORATE PLANNING

There are five steps in corporate planning. As can be seen from Table 2-2, the starting point is usually a statement of corporate financial objectives

TABLE 2-2 Marketing Planning and its Place in the Corporate Cycle

Step 1: Corporate Financial Objectives	Step 2: Management Audit	Step 3: Objective and Strategy Setting	Step 4: Plans	Step 5: Corporate Plans
Targeted growth in sales and earnings	Marketing audit	Marketing objectives, strategies	Marketing plan	
	Distribution audit	Distribution objectives, strategies	Distribution plan	
	Manufacturing audit	Manufacturing objectives, strategies	Manufacturing plan	Issue of corporate plan, to include corporate objectives and strategies; marketing objectives and strategies, etc.
	Financial audit	Financial objectives, strategies	Financial plan	
	Personnel audit	Personnel objectives, strategies	Human resource plan	

for long-range planning, which are often expressed in terms of sales, profit before tax, and return on investment.

More often than not, this long-range planning horizon is five years away, although three years is becoming the norm. The precise period is determined by the nature of the markets in which the company operates. For example, five years is not long enough for a glass manufacturer, because it takes that long to commission a new furnace, whereas in the fashion industry, five years is too long.

For the purpose of allowing sufficient detail for a strategic plan to be of practical use, it is advisable to keep the period down to three years if possible. Beyond this period, detail of any kind is likely to become pointless. There can certainly be scenarios of five to ten years and longer, but not a plan in the sense intended herein.

The next step is the *management audit,* which we have already discussed. A thorough situation review, particularly in the area of marketing, enables the company to determine whether it can reach long-range financial targets with its current range of products in its current markets. Any projected gap must be filled by product development or market extension.

Objective and strategy setting: do it properly. Undoubtedly the most important and difficult of all stages in corporate planning is the third step, *objective and strategy setting.* If this is not done properly, everything that follows is of little value.

Later we discuss marketing objectives and strategies in detail. For now, the important point is that this is the time in the planning cycle when a compromise has to be reached between what is wanted by the several functional departments and what is practicable, given all the constraints in any company. For example, it is not good to set a marketing objective of penetrating a new market if the company does not have the production capacity to cope with the new business and if capital is not available for the investment necessary. At this stage, objectives and strategies are set for three years or for whatever the planning horizon is.

The fourth step involves producing detailed *plans* for one year that contain the responsibilities, timing and costs of achieving the first year's objectives, and broad plans for the following years. These plans can then be incorporated into the *corporate plan,* which contains long-range corporate objectives, strategies, plans, profit and loss accounts, and balance sheets.

A corporate plan provides the long-term vision of what you are striving to achieve with your strategy.

One of the main purposes of a corporate plan is to provide a long-term vision of what the company is or is striving to become, taking into account shareholder expectations, environmental trends, resource market trends, consumption market trends, and the distinctive competence of the company as revealed by the management audit. What this means in practice is that the corporate plan usually contains at least the following elements:

1. The desired level of profitability
2. Business boundaries
   - What kinds of products will be sold to what kinds of markets (marketing)
   - What kinds of facilities will be developed (production and distribution)
   - The size and character of the labor force (personnel)
   - Funding (finance)
   - Technologies to be developed (research and development)
3. Other corporate objectives, such as social responsibility, corporate, stock market, and employer image

Such a corporate plan, which contains projected profit and loss statements and balance sheets, is more likely to provide long-term stability for a company than plans based on an intuitive process that contain forecasts that tend to be little more than extrapolations of previous trends.

The headquarters of one major multinational company with a sophisticated budgeting system used to receive "plans" from all over the world and coordinate them in quantitative and cross-functional terms such as numbers of employees, units of sales, items of plant, and square feet of production area, together with the associated financial implications. The trouble was that the whole complicated edifice was built on the initial sales forecasts, which were themselves little more than a time-consuming numbers game. The key strategic issues relating to products and markets were lost in all the financial activity, which eventually resulted in serious operational and profitability problems.

ASSUMPTIONS

Let us now return to the preparation of the marketing plan. All companies have key determinants of success about which assumptions have to be made before the planning process can proceed. It is a question of stand-

Examples of Corporate Assumptions

With respect to the industrial climate of the company, the following is assumed:

Industrial overcapacity will increase from 105 percent to 115 percent as new plants come into operation.

Price competition will force price levels down by 10 percent across the board.

A new product that competes with our product x will be introduced by our major competitor before the end of the second quarter.

ardizing the planning environment. For example, it would not be helpful to receive plans from two product managers, one of whom believed the market was going to increase by 10 percent while the other believed the market was going to decline by 10 percent. Assumptions should be few in number. If a plan is possible irrespective of the assumptions made, then the assumptions are unnecessary.

MARKETING OBJECTIVES AND STRATEGIES

The next step in marketing planning is the writing of marketing objectives and strategies, the key step in the entire process. An *objective* is what you want to achieve. A *strategy* is how you plan to achieve your objectives. There can be objectives and strategies at all levels in marketing. For example, there can be advertising objectives and strategies and pricing objectives and strategies. The important point about marketing objectives is that they are about *products* and *markets* only. Marketing objectives are about one or more of the following:

- Existing products in existing markets
- New products for existing markets
- Existing products for new markets
- New products for new markets

Marketing objectives can be measured. Directional terms such as "maximize," "minimize," "penetrate," and "increase," are acceptable only if quantitative measurement can be attached to them. Measurement is expressed in terms of some, or all, of the following: sales volume, sales value, market share, profit, percentage penetration of outlets, awareness and esteem.

TABLE 2-3 The Marketing Mix

Product	The general policies for product deletions, modifications, additions, design, packaging, etc.
Price	The general pricing policies to be followed for product groups in market segments.
Place	The general policies for channels and customer service levels.
Promotion	The general policies for communicating with customers via advertising, personal selling, sales promotion, public relations, marketing public relations, direct marketing via mail, telephone, the internet, and exhibitions.

Marketing strategies are the means by which marketing objectives are achieved and expressed in the *marketing mix* as outlined in Table 2-3.

THE MARKETING MIX

The heart of the marketing plan is expressed in the marketing mix. The mix is the set of controllable variables in the marketing plan that are usually expressed as the four Ps—product, price, place, and promotion. The challenge in marketing planning is to optimize the mix by adjusting each variable and the budget for each variable to maximize the value for customers and the contribution to the firm measured in sales and profits or any other organizational goal.

For example, raising a price increases revenue per unit and either depresses or increases total revenue depending on demand elasticity for the product. Demand elasticity depends on the quantity and quality of advertising and other forms of communication and the features and benefits of the product itself. In the early part of 1996, Ford Motor Company appeared to have overestimated the price elasticity of demand for its cars when it added features and engineering refinements that raised Ford's prices above those of its direct competitors, who offered less engineering refinement, fewer features, and a lower price in competition with Ford. Chevrolet engaged in direct-comparison advertising that focused on basic features and the Chevrolet price advantage and succeeded in taking market share from Ford.

Each strategy must be costed out to determine practicability. In this exercise, assumptions concerning market response must be combined with estimates of required expenditure to arrive at feasible alternatives.

**The plan deter-
mines where
the company is
now, where it
wants to go,
and how to get
there; it should
be the backdrop
against which
all organiza-
tional decisions
are made.**

USE OF MARKETING PLANS

The marketing plan normally includes an advertising plan, a sales promotion plan, a pricing plan, a distribution plan, a product plan, and a target
market plan that addresses objectives and targets by market segment. A
written strategic marketing plan is the reference against which operational decisions are made on an ongoing basis. Detail is not the goal. The
main function of the marketing plan is to determine where the company
is now, where it wants to go, and how to get there. The marketing plan
lies at the heart of a company's revenue-generating activities. From the
plan flow all other corporate activities, such as timing of cash flow and
size and character of the labor force.

THE MARKETING BUDGET

The best budgeting is to justify all marketing expenditures from a zero
base each year against the tasks that you wish to accomplish. If these procedures are followed, every item of budgeted expenditure can be related
directly back to the corporate objectives. For example, if sales promotion
is an important means of achieving an objective in a particular market,
when sales promotional items appear in the program, each one has a specific purpose that can be related to a main objective. This method ensures
that every item of expenditure is fully accounted for as part of a rational,
objective, and task approach. It also ensures that when changes have to be
made they can be made in such a way that the least damage is caused to
the company's long-term objectives.

WHAT SHOULD APPEAR IN A STRATEGIC
MARKETING PLAN?

The marketing plan lies at the heart of a company's revenue-generating
activities. A written strategic marketing plan is a guide for operational decisions. Extreme detail is avoided. The function of the plan is to determine
where the company is, where it wants to go, and how it can get there.
What should actually appear in a written strategic marketing plan is
shown in Figure 2-3. Details and explanations of each of the components
are provided later.

WHAT IS A MISSION OR PURPOSE STATEMENT?

A mission statement is one of the most difficult aspects of marketing planning to master, largely because it is philosophical and qualitative in nature. Many organizations find different departments, and sometimes even different groups in the same department, pulling in different directions, often with disastrous results, simply because the organization has not defined the boundaries of the business and the way it wishes to do business.

The following should appear in a mission or purpose statement, which should normally consist of no more than one paragraph:

1. Role or contribution
   * Profit (specify)
   * Service
   * Opportunity seeker
2. Business definition—define the business in terms of the *benefits* you provide or the *needs* you satisfy, rather than in terms of what you make.
3. Core competencies—identify the essential skills, capabilities, and resources that are the keys to future success. Core competence is an integration of skills and technologies, not a single skill. It must be competitively unique so as to provide competitor advantage. If you can equally well put a competitor's name to competencies, they are merely baseline capabilities and are not core competencies.
4. The unique and valuable position that the company has chosen to take in the marketplace.
5. Indications for the future
   * What the firm *will* do
   * What the firm *might* do
   * What the firm will *never* do

Three Types of Mission Statements

Type 1 A motherhood statement usually found in annual reports designed to stroke shareholders, otherwise of no practical use.

Type 2 The real thing. A meaningful statement, unique to the organization concerned that influences the efforts of everyone in the organization.

Type 3 A purpose statement (or lower level mission statement). Appropriate at the strategic business unit, departmental, or product group level of the organization.

The logical sequence of events, then, leading to the setting of marketing objectives and the formation of plans for achieving them is to write a mission statement, set corporate objectives, conduct the marketing audit, conduct the SWOT analysis, make assumptions, set marketing objectives and strategies, estimate expected results, identify alternative plans and mixes, set the budget, and establish the first year's implementation program. The following chapters give details on how to perform these tasks. As business becomes increasingly complex and competition increases, a marketing plan is essential.

QUESTIONS SUCCESSFUL COMPANIES ASK

1. How do we see the logical sequence of events leading to the establishment of our marketing objectives?
2. How can we successfully achieve each of the steps in the market plan sequence?
3. What should our plan contain and how shall we use it?
4. Why should we do this? Does it create a unique value for our customers?

3 The Marketing Audit: Customers and Markets

This chapter focuses specifically on to whom one sells, and chapter 4 focuses on what one sells to them. The other elements of marketing are covered in chapters 6 through 10. We begin by defining the difference between customers and consumers, the meaning of market share, and the meaning of Pareto analysis. We then describe market segmentation and the several methods of segmenting markets, including customer behavior, benefit analysis, and customer attitudes. Examples of market segmentation are provided. The chapter closes by emphasizing why market segmentation is vital to marketing planning.

When you understand the process of marketing planning, you can begin to look in more detail at its principal components. You have, as it were, seen the picture on the jigsaw puzzle; now you can examine the individual pieces with a better understanding of where they fit.

The next two chapters are designed to help perform a meaningful marketing audit. We have already discussed the issues to be considered; now you need the tools to undertake such an analysis. The contents of the strategic marketing plan, outlined in chapter 2, represent the conclusions from the marketing audit and are only as good as the audit allows. The marketing audit is a separate step in the process, and under no circumstances do voluminous data and analysis appear in the plan. The marketing audit is a crucial stage in the marketing planning process. Do not confuse it with the marketing plan itself, the actual contents of which are set out in detail in chapter 12.

THE DIFFERENCE BETWEEN CUSTOMERS AND CONSUMERS

One of the key determinants of successful marketing planning is *market segmentation*. This is fundamental to the matching process described in chapter 1. To understand market segmentation, it is first necessary to appreciate the difference between *customers* and *consumers*, the meaning of *market share*, and the phenomenon known as the *Pareto effect*.

31

A fertilizer company with a product advantage prospered during the 1970s and 1980s, using distributors to reach its farmer consumers. However, as other companies copied the company's technology, distributors began to carry competitive products and drove prices and margins down. Had it paid more attention to the needs of its different farmer groups and developed products especially for them, on the basis of farmer segmentation, the company would have continued to create demand through differentiation. As it was, the company's products became commodities, and the power shifted almost entirely to the distributors. This company is no longer in business. There are countless other examples of companies that did not pay sufficient attention to the needs of users farther down the value chain. They eventually ceased to provide any real value to their direct customers and went out of business.

Consumers may not necessarily be your customers. Start with the difference between customers and consumers. The final consumer is not necessarily the customer. Take the example of a mother buying breakfast cereals. The chances are she is an intermediate *customer*, acting as agent on behalf of the *consumers* (her family). To market cereals effectively, it is necessary to understand what the end-consumer wants as well as what the parents want.

When you appreciate the distinction between customers and consumers and the need to be constantly alert to any changes in the ultimate consumption patterns of products, the next question is, Who are our customers? Direct customers are people or organizations who actually buy directly from you. They can be distributors, retailers, and the like. However, as intimated in the previous paragraph, there is a tendency for organizations to confine their interest, and thus their marketing, only to those who actually place orders. This can be a mistake, as can be seen from the case history above.

MARKET SHARE

Closely related to the question of the difference between customers and consumers is the question of what our market share is. Most business people already understand that there is a direct relation between a relatively high share of any market and high returns on investment. It is important to be most careful about how *market* is defined. For example, SMH, a Swiss company, sells many different brands of watches, including Omega and Swatch. Although both Omega and Swatch are watches, they are not in the same market. The Omega is in the luxury jewelry market, and the Swatch is in the fashion accessory market. Correct market definition is crucial for measurement of market share and market growth, specification of target customers, reconfirmation of relevant competitors, and, most important of all, formulation of a marketing strategy that delivers differential advantage.

Market = aggregation of all the products that appear to satisfy the same *need*.

The general rule for market definition is that it is the aggregation of all the products that appear to satisfy the same need. For example, the in-company caterer is regarded as only one option when it comes to satisfying lunchtime hunger. This particular need also can be satisfied at restaurants, fast food outlets, and delicatessens. The emphasis in the definition, therefore, is clearly on the word *need*.

It is important to arrive at a meaningful balance between a broad market definition and a manageable market definition. Too narrow a definition has the pitfall of restricting the range of new opportunities and segments that can open up for your business. On the other hand, too broad a definition may make marketing planning meaningless. For example, the television broadcasting companies are in the *entertainment* market, which also consists of theaters, cinemas, and theme parks, to name but a few. This is a fairly broad definition. Therefore, it may be more manageable for television broadcasters, when looking at segmenting their market, to define their market as being the *home information and entertainment* market. This could be further refined into the *preschool, child, teenager, family, or adult home information and entertainment* market.

To help with calculating market share, the following definitions are useful:

- **Product class** cigarettes, computers, fuel, earth-moving equipment
- **Product subclass** filter, personal computers, gasoline, crawler tractors
- **Product brand** Marlboro, Compaq, Mobil, Caterpillar

Coke as a brand, for the purpose of measuring market share, is concerned only with *the aggregate of all other brands that satisfy the same group of customer wants.* Nevertheless, the Coca-Cola company also needs to be aware of the sales trends of all beverages.

One of the most frequent mistakes made by people who do not understand what market share really means is to assume that their company has only a small share of a product class or subclass market. If the company is successful, it probably has a much larger share of a segment of one of these broader markets. For example, Psion, a company in the United Kingdom with sales of $150 million, has a trivial share of the computer market. For handheld computers weighing less than two pounds, in 1996 Psion had an impressive 34 percent share of the world market, which made the company number one in the world in this segment.

Although it is tempting to believe that the foregoing examples amount to "rigging" the definition of market and that there is a danger of fooling ourselves, never lose sight of the purpose of market segmentation, which is to provide one's company with a competitive advantage by providing greater value to customers. A New York orchestra may define its market as the audiences served by aggregation of all New York classical orchestras rather than as all entertainment. The key is that a market definition enables it to outperform its competitors and grow profitably. The definition must be continuously reviewed and revised.

To summarize, correct market definition is crucial for the following purposes:

- Share measurement
- Growth measurement
- Specification of target customers
- Recognition of relevant competitors
- Formulation of marketing objectives and strategies

This brings us to another useful and fascinating observation about markets.

PARETO EFFECT

It is a phenomenon commonly observed by most companies that a small proportion of their customers account for a large proportion of their business. This is often referred to as the 80/20 rule, or the Pareto effect, whereby about 20 percent of customers account for about 80 percent of business.

A graph of the proportion of customers who account for a certain proportion of sales may provide the relation similar to that in Figure 3-1. Here, customers have been categorized simply as A, B, or C according to the proportion of sales for which they account. The A customers, perhaps 25 percent of the total, account for about 70 percent of sales; B customers, about 55 percent of the total, account for 20 percent of total sales; and C customers, 20 percent of the total, account for the remaining 10 percent of sales.

The Pareto effect is found in all markets, from capital industrial goods to financial services to consumer goods. The implication of this fact about markets is clear: marketers need to focus efforts and programs on high-volume customers. One of the most important tasks in marketing plan-

Figure 3-1
*Pareto Effect: Log
Normal Distribu-
tion*

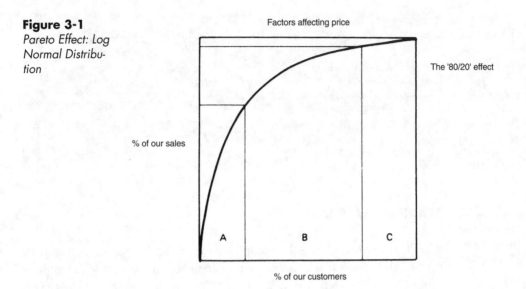

ning is being able to choose the best 20 percent of your market and focus on that. A method for doing this is provided in chapter 5.

MARKET SEGMENTATION

Failure to understand the importance of market segmentation is the principal reason for failure to compete effectively in world markets.

We can now begin to concentrate on a method for making market segmentation a reality. Markets usually fall into natural groups, or segments, that contain customers who exhibit the same broad characteristics. These segments form separate markets in themselves and can often be of considerable size. Taken to its extreme, each individual consumer is a unique market segment, for all people are different in their requirements. However, it is clearly uneconomical to make unique products for the needs of individuals. Products are made to appeal to groups of customers who share approximately the same needs.

Unless you succeed in identifying a viable market segment for your product, you will not achieve differential advantage and will become just another company selling "me too" products. There are basically three steps to market segmentation. The first is measuring customer behavior and answering the question *who* is buying *what*? The second answers the question *why* are they buying what they buy? The third step involves searching and identifying market segments.

Market segments have the following characteristics:

- Segments should be of an adequate size to provide the company with the desired return for its effort.
- Members of each segment should have a high degree of similarity, yet be distinct from the rest of the market.

- Criteria for describing segments must be relevant to the purchase situation.
- Segments must be reachable, that is, they must respond to a distinctive marketing mix.

MARKET MAPPING

Few companies can be "all things to all people."

A useful way of tackling the complex issue of market segmentation is to start by drawing a *market map* as a precursor to a more detailed examination of who buys what. A market map defines the value chain between supplier and final user, which takes into account the various buying mechanisms found in a market, including the part played by *influencers*. In general, if an organization's products or services go through the same channels to similar end users, one composite market map can be drawn. If, however, some products or services go through totally different channels or to totally different markets, more than one market map is needed.

Business units normally are mapped individually because such structures usually exist because the volume or value of business justifies a specific focus. For example, in the case of a farming cooperative that supplies seeds, fertilizer, crop protection, insurance, and banking to farmers, it would be sensible to start by drawing a separate market map for each of these product groups, even though they all appear to go through similar channels to the same end users. In other words, start the mapping (and subsequent segmentation) process at the lowest level of disaggregation within the current structure of the organization.

Track your products and services right through to the end user.

An example of a very basic market map is shown in Figure 3-2. It is very important that your market map tracks your products and services along with those of your competitors all the way through to the final users, even though you may not actually sell directly to them.

In some markets, the direct customer-purchaser will not always be the final user. For example, a company (or household) may commission a third party contractor to provide some redecoration, or an advertising agency to develop and conduct a promotional campaign, or a bank, accountant, or financial adviser to produce and implement a financial program. The physician you visit when seeking treatment is, in many respects, a contractor when it comes to prescribing medicine. Although

Figure 3-2
A Simple Market Map

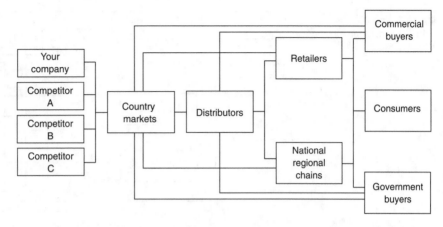

Note: This market map combines domestic and business-to-business end users. Some of the distribution channels are common to both of them.

the contractor specifies the product (the drug prescription), he or she is not the final user. The distinction is important; to win the assignment the contractor has to understand the requirements of the customer. To leave the final user out of the market map therefore ignores an array of different needs of which the supplier must be aware (and include in the product offer) if the supplier is to ensure the company name appears on the contractor's *preferred supplier list.* The inclusion of a contractor on a market map is illustrated in Figure 3-3.

So far we have mapped out the different transactions that take place in a market all the way through to the final user and have shown how the transactions relate to each other. By quantifying the various routes and determining your company's share along them, you identify the most important routes and your company's position along each of them.

By looking at when decisions are made between the products or services of competing suppliers, you identify a number of stages (junctions) at which segmentation can occur. For most companies, we recommend that segmentation first take place at the junction farthest away from the supplier and manufacturer; it is at this junction that decisions are made.

WHO BUYS

A useful method for dealing with this stage of market segmentation is to refer to the market map and at each point at which there is a critical purchase influence attempt to describe the characteristics of the customers

Figure 3-3
*Market Map with
Contractor*

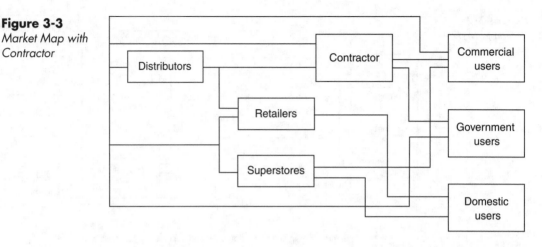

Note: In this particular market map the introduction of contractors has now reduced the similarity between the domestic and business-to-business end users quite notably. Superstores continue to be shared with a proportion of the commercial users, but this new contractor stage only operates in a business-to-business field.

who belong to the segment. The descriptions can consist of a single characteristic or a combination, whichever is appropriate to the market being analyzed.

Analyze your customer's attributes.
Analysis of customer attributes is important in helping to design a communication program. This is when analysis of customer attributes becomes important. It is used to find a way to describe the customer groups identified in the previous analysis for the purpose of communicating with them. However clever you may be in isolating segments, unless you can find a way to describe the segments to address them through a communication program, the efforts are to no avail. Demographic descriptors are the most useful method for this purpose. For consumer markets, these descriptors are income, age, sex, education, stage in the family life cycle, nationality, and socioeconomic group.

WHAT IS BOUGHT

When you look at what is bought, the value of the market map becomes apparent. We are really talking about the actual structure of markets in the form of volume, value, the physical characteristics of products, place of purchase, frequency of purchase, price paid, and so on. This tells you, if there are any groups of products (or outlets, or price categories) that are growing, static, or declining, that is where the opportunities are and where the problems are. Analysis of product and purchase characteristics tells how the market works and helps one understand the market structure.

For example, a carpet company whose sales were declining found during analysis that although the market in total was rising, the particular outlets to which they had traditionally sold were accounting for a declining proportion of total market sales. Furthermore, demand for higher priced products was falling, as was demand for the particular fiber types manufactured by this company. All this added up to a decline in sales and profitability and led the company to re-target its efforts on the growing sectors of the market.

This is market segmentation at its most elementary level, yet it is surprising to find even today how many companies run apparently sophisticated budgeting systems based on little more than crude extrapolations of past sales trends and that leave the marketing strategies implicit. Such systems are usually the ones that cause serious problems when market structures change, as in the case of the carpet company.

The next task is to list *all* relevant competitive products and services whether or not you manufacture them. Make sure that you unbundle all the components of a purchase so that you arrive at a comprehensive list of *what is bought*. Also, draw up a list that covers the different frequencies of purchase experienced for your own, and your competitors', products and services.

Next, draw up a separate list covering the different methods of purchase and, if applicable, the different purchasing organizations and procedures observed in your market. For example:

- **Methods of payment** credit cards, direct debit, cash, check
- **Type of purchase** switch, rebuy, new purchase
- **Purchasing organization** centralized, decentralized, buying influencers, decision makers

Next, attempt to identify for each active *who* all the unique combinations of *what is bought* observed in their particular buying activity. The resulting cascade produces a large number of microsegments, each of which has a volume or value figure attached. These can be reduced in number by determining the important from the unimportant and by removing anything that is obviously superfluous.

Some preliminary screening at this stage is vital to cut this long list down to manageable proportions. This also acts as a preliminary form of market segmentation.

Target your efforts on your most promising opportunities.

WHY CUSTOMERS BUY

The second part of analyzing customer behavior is trying to understand why customers behave the way they do. If we can explain the behavior of our customers, we are in a better position to sell to them.

The most useful and practical way of explaining customer behavior is benefit segmentation, that is, the benefits sought by customers when they buy a product. For example, some customers buy products for functional characteristics (product), for economy (price), for convenience and availability (place), for emotional reasons (promotion), or for a combination of these reasons (a trade-off). Understanding the benefits sought by customers helps organize the marketing mix in the way most likely to appeal to the target market. The importance of product benefits is clarified in chapter 4 in the discussion of product management.

Customers don't buy products; they seek to acquire benefits. Behind this statement lies a basic principle of successful marketing. When people purchase products, they are not motivated in the first instance by physical features or objective attributes of the product but by the benefit that those attributes bring with them. To take an example from industrial marketing, a purchaser of industrial cutting oil is not buying the particular blend of chemicals sold by leading manufacturers of industrial lubricants; he is buying a bundle of benefits that include the solution to a specific lubrication problem.

The difference between benefits and products is not simply a question of semantics. It is crucial to the company seeking success. Every product has its features, such as size, shape, performance, weight, and the material from which it is made. Many companies fall into the trap of talking to customers about these features rather than about what the features mean to the customer. This is not surprising. For example, if a salesperson asked a question about a product cannot provide an accurate answer, the customer might lose confidence and, doubting the salesperson, soon doubt the product. Most salespeople, therefore, are very knowledgeable about the technical features of the products they sell. They have to have these details at their fingertips when they talk to buyers, designers, and technical experts.

Being expert in technical detail, however, is not enough. The customer may not be able to see the benefits that particular features bring. It is therefore up to the salesperson to explain the benefits that accrue from every feature mentioned. A simple formula to ensure that this customer-oriented approach is adopted is always to use the phrase "which means that" to link a feature to the benefit it brings, as follows:

Maintenance time has been reduced from 4 to 3 hours, *which means that* most costs are reduced by . . .

The new special bearing has self-aligning symmetric rollers, *which means that* the rollers find their own equilibrium with the load always symmetrically distributed along the length of the roller, *which means* an extended life capacity of one year on average.

BENEFITS ANALYSIS

A company must undertake a detailed analysis to determine the full range of benefits it has to offer its customers. This can be done by listing the features of major products with what they mean to the customer. The analysis produces various classes of benefits.

Standard Benefits

Standard benefits are the basic benefits that arise from the features of the company and its products. Every benefit must be listed. Care is needed to produce a comprehensive list. Because company staff are familiar with the company and its products, they may take some features for granted. Take care not to fall into this trap when providing a benefit analysis.

Double Benefits

A company often can identify double benefits. For example, it may be selling a product that benefits the customer and, by means of improvement in the customer's product, the end-user. For example, our fax, copier, printer, scanner model performs four tasks, *which means that:*

- The product will appeal to a wide variety of customers
- Users save space and money
- We offer a unique value for the small business customer

In the example, the first benefit applies to the customer because it widens the customer's potential market and the additional benefits apply to the potential end-user.

Company Benefits

Customers rarely simply buy products; they buy a relationship with the supplier. Factors such as delivery, credit, after-sales service, location of depots and offices, and reputation are relevant to the customer. The benefit analysis therefore examines the company and the back-up services it offers. Typical company benefits are as follows:

We offer a twenty-four hour service because we have a national network of deliverers, *which means that* you will never lose production because of down time.

We are a large international corporation, *which means that* you can rely on comprehensive service throughout the world.

You can be sure of individual attention from us because we are a small family business.

Differential Benefits

Although it is important for the salesperson to conduct the benefit analysis most thoroughly, it is vital in the analysis that differential benefits compared with those of chief competitors be identified. If a company cannot identify any differential benefits, either what they are offering is identical to its competitors' offerings (which is unlikely) or the company has not conducted the benefit analysis properly. It is in differential benefits that the greatest chance of success lies.

BRINGING IT ALL TOGETHER

The segmentation is almost complete. The second step involves taking each cluster identified earlier (who buys and what they buy) and listing why they buy. In other words, what benefits are customers seeking by buying what they buy?

The third and final step is to look for *clusters* of segments that share similar needs and to apply to the resulting clusters the organization's minimum volume and value criteria to determine viability. This final step can be difficult and time-consuming, but care lavished on this part of the market segmentation process pays handsome dividends at later stages of the marketing planning process.

Summary of Bases for Market Segmentation

What is bought	Price
	Outlets
	Physical characteristics
	Geography
Who buys	Demographic
	Socioeconomic
	Brand loyalty
	Heavy or light user
	Personality traits, life-style
Why	Benefits
	Attitudes
	Perceptions
	Preferences

WHY MARKET SEGMENTATION IS VITAL IN MARKETING PLANNING

In today's highly competitive world, few companies can afford to compete only on price. The product has not yet been sold that someone, some-where, cannot sell less expensively. In many markets it is rarely the least expensive product that succeeds anyway. This issue is discussed in chapter 8, "The Pricing Plan." You have to find a way to differentiate yourself from the competition; the answer is market segmentation.

The truth is that few companies can afford to be all things to all people. The main aim of market segmentation as part of planning is to enable a firm to aim its efforts at the most promising opportunities. But what is an opportunity for firm A is not necessarily an opportunity for firm B. So a firm needs to develop a *typology* of the customer or segment it prefers; this can be an instrument of great productivity in the marketplace. The typology of the customer or the segment can be based on a myriad of criteria, such as the following:

- Size of the firm
- Consumption level of the firm
- Nature of the firm's products, production, or processes
- Motivation of the decision-makers (e.g., desire to deal with large firms)
- Geographic location

The point of segmentation is that a company must do one of the following:

- Define its markets broadly enough to ensure that the costs for key activities are competitive
- Define its markets in such a way that it can offer unique value to customers

Both tasks have to be related to a firm's *distinctive competence* and to that of its competitors.

All this comes to the fore as a result of the marketing audit and is summarized in SWOT (strengths, weaknesses, opportunities, and threats) analysis. In particular, the differential benefits of a firm's product or service should be beyond doubt to all key members of the company. Even more important than this, however, is the issue of marketing planning and all that follows in this book. It is worth repeating why market segmentation is so important. Correct market definition is crucial for the following:

- Share measurement
- Growth measurement
- Specification of target customers
- Recognition of relevant competitors
- Formulation of marketing objectives and strategies

The typology of the customer or the market segment must be related to your firm's distinctive competence.

Segmentation is not something a company can do once and forget. Because markets and customers are constantly changing, segments constantly change. Table 3-1 shows what happens to a company that treats segments as fixed points rather than as constantly evolving targets. In 1921, General Motors brands were differentiated and focused on distinctive target markets. By 1996, these same brands had lost their distinctive price positioning in the market place. The market had shifted from a segmentation based on price and size to one based on multiple factors, including lifestyle and vehicle category. Price was still a factor but one of many factors. General Motors' powerful 1921 price and size brand segmentation is more of a drag than a lift in the markets of the 1990s and beyond.

To summarize, the objectives of market segmentation are as follows:

- To help determine how best to focus the firm's resources and efforts to create differential advantage and customer value

TABLE 3-1 GM's Sad Decline

1921		1996	
Brands positioned along different price points		No focus or position; all brands in the center of the market	
Chevrolet	$450 to $600	Saturn	$9,995 to $12,895
Pontiac	$600 to $900	Chevrolet	$7,295 to $67,543
Oldsmobile	$900 to $1,200	Pontiac	$9,904 to $26,479
Buick	$1,200 to $1,700	Oldsmobile	$13,510 to $31,370
Cadillac	$1,700 to $ 2,500	Buick	$13,734 to $31,864
		Cadillac	$32,990 to $45,330

Source: Trout, Jack, with Steve Rivkin, *The New Positioning: The Latest on the World's #1 Business Strategy.* New York: McGraw-Hill, 1996, p. 52.

- To help determine realistic and achievable marketing and sales objectives
- To improve decision making by forcing managers to consider in depth the options ahead

QUESTIONS SUCCESSFUL COMPANIES ASK

1. Are we serving customers or consumers?
2. How do we define our market?
3. What is our market share?
4. Who are our most important competitors?
5. Why do our customers buy what they buy and why do they buy from us?
6. How is our market changing? What are the new segments we need to address?

4 The Marketing Audit: Products

Chapter 4 defines what a product is, product life cycle analysis, and the Boston Consulting Group (BCG) matrix. It outlines certain weaknesses in the BCG matrix approach and introduces the directional policy matrix as a tool of analysis. The chapter outlines the types of information needed about products as part of the marketing audit and presents a number of fundamental diagnostic marketing tools.

WHAT IS A PRODUCT?

The central role of the product in marketing management makes it such an important subject that mismanagement in this area is unlikely to be compensated by good management in other areas.

The vital aspects of product management discussed in this chapter are the nature of products, product life cycles, the concept of the product portfolio, and new product development. The purpose of this discussion is to help in the performance of a product audit to set meaningful marketing objectives. Before a discussion of product management, it is necessary to understand what a product is, because this is the root of misunderstanding about product management.

A product is a problem solver in the sense that it solves the customer's problems. It is also the means by which the company achieves its objectives. The clue to what constitutes a product can be found in an examination of what it is that customers appear to buy. For example, Theodore Levitt, the famous marketing guru, points out that what customers *want* when they buy one-quarter inch drills is one-quarter inch holes. In other words the drill itself is only a means to an end. The lesson here for the drill manufacturer is that if the company really believes its business is the manufacture of drills rather than the manufacture of the means of making holes in materials, it is in grave danger of going out of business as soon as a better means of making holes is invented, such as, for example, a pocket laser.

A company that fails to think of its business in terms of customer benefits rather than in terms of physical products or services is in danger

47

of losing its competitive position in the market. This is why so much attention is paid in chapter 3 to the subject of benefit analysis.

So far, we have not said much about service products, such as consulting, banking, and insurance. The reason for this is simply that, as stated in chapter 1, the marketing of services is not very different from the marketing of goods. The greatest difference is that a service product has benefits that cannot be stored. An airline seat, for example, if not used at the time of the flight, is gone forever, whereas a physical product may be stored and used at a later date.

The marketing of services is not very different from the marketing of goods.

In practice, this disadvantage makes little difference in marketing terms. The problem seems to lie in the difficulty many service product companies have in perceiving and presenting their offerings as *products.* Consider the example of the consultant. The world is full of a constantly changing army of people who set themselves up as consultants, and it is not unusual to see people presenting themselves, for example, as general marketing consultants. It would be difficult for any prospective client to glean from such a description exactly what benefits this person is offering. Yet the market for consulting is no different from any other market. It is a simple matter to segment the market and develop products that deliver the particular package of benefits desired.

When customers buy products, even as an industrial buyer purchasing a piece of equipment for a company, they are still buying a particular bundle of benefits perceived as satisfying their own particular needs and wants. This is illustrated in Figure 4-1.

There is a great danger in leaving product decisions to engineers and scientists. If these people are not market driven they focus on the formal product and ignore the core benefit or service and the augmented product, which may account for as much as 80 percent or more of the customer value in a product.

IMPORTANCE OF THE BRAND

A brand is an identity that communicates a promise about the benefits of a product. Brand identity is created by one or more of the following elements: a name, a logo, a symbol, color, type fonts, package design, and the design or look of the product itself. The three-pointed star hood ornament on the Mercedes Benz is part of the Mercedes brand identity, just as the five-pointed star on a pair of sneakers is part of the brand identity of Converse, an athletic shoe company that has been in business for more than 75 years.

Figure 4-1

Three Dimensions of a Product

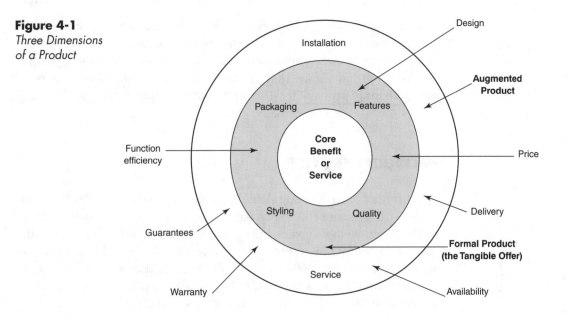

A company name may be a brand. Company brands are referred to as umbrella or banner brands: IBM, Intel, and Sony are examples. A product brand is an identity created for a single product or product line. Marlboro, Tide, and Jello are examples of product brands.

Company and brand names secure relationships with customers.

Most people are aware of the Coca-Cola–Pepsi Cola blind taste tests, in which blinded consumers showed a definite preference for Pepsi. When the labels were revealed, however, 65 percent of consumers claimed to prefer Coca-Cola. This is a clear indication of the value of the *product surround*. That product surround is an important determinant of commercial success there can be little doubt. When one company buys another, as in the case of Ford and Jaguar, it is frequently true that the value of the acquisition is not the tangible assets that appear on the balance sheet, such as plant and equipment, but the *brand names* owned by the company being acquired.

It is also a fact that whenever brand names are neglected, what is known as the *commodity slide* begins. This is because the physical characteristics of products are becoming increasingly difficult to differentiate and easy to emulate. When products are in a slide category, purchase decisions tend to be made on the basis of price or availability.

Business history is replete with examples of strong brand names that have been allowed to decay through lack of attention, often because of a lack of both promotion and continuous product-improvement programs. The difference between a brand and a commodity can be summed up in the term *added values,* which are the additional attributes, or intangibles, that the consumer perceives as being embodied in the product. A product with a strong brand name is more than the sum of its component parts.

Research has shown that perceived product quality is an important determinant of profitability. This issue is discussed in chapter 5 in the section "Competitive Strategies."

PRODUCT LIFE CYCLE

Product life cycle is the postulate that if a new product is successful at the introductory stage (and many fail at this point), then repeat purchase gradually grows and spreads and the rate of sales growth increases. At this stage, competitors often enter the market, and their additional promotional expenditures further expand the market. But no market is infinitely expandable, and eventually the *rate* of growth slows as the product moves into its maturity stage. The point eventually is reached at which there are too many firms in the market, price wars break out, some firms drop out of the market, and finally the market itself falls into decline. Figure 4-2 illustrates these apparently universal phenomena.

Although the product life cycle may well be a useful practical generalization for a product category, specific product brand life cycles are determined more by the activities of the company than by any underlying law. For example, Marlboro cigarettes, although exhibiting all the characteristics of the classic product life cycle, recorded new sales heights after the decision in the 1950s to reposition the brand from a women's cigarette to a cigarette for anyone who identified with the archetype of freedom. Had this repositioning not been made, the brand would probably have gone into decline.

From a management point of view, the product life cycle concept is useful in that it focuses attention on the future sales pattern that is likely

Figure 4-2
Product Life Cycle

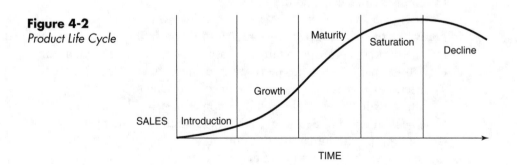

if no corrective action is taken. Several courses of action are open to maintain the profitable sales of a product over its life cycle.

The implications of the product life cycle concept are important in every element of the marketing mix. Figure 4-3 gives a guide to how a product has to change over its life cycle. In addition to this, however, every other element also has to change. For example, if a company rigidly adheres to a premium pricing policy at the mature stage of the product life cycle, when markets are often overcrowded and price wars begin, it loses market share unless it repositions itself as a luxury or premium-priced product.

The same applies to promotion. During the early phase of product introduction, the task of advertising is to create awareness. During the growth phase the task may be to change to creation of a favorable attitude toward the product. The policy toward channels should not be fixed. At first one is concerned with distribution of the product in the most important channels. During the growth phase one has to consider ways of reaching the new channels that want the product.

Drawing a product life cycle can be extremely difficult, even with time series analysis. This is connected with the complex question of measurement of market share.

A firm needs to be concerned with its share (or its proportion of volume or value) of an *actual* market, rather than with a *potential* market. One of the most frequent mistakes made by companies that do not under-

Figure 4-3

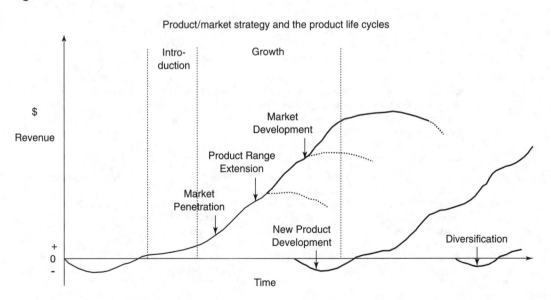

51

TABLE 4-1 Guide to Market Maturity

Maturity Stage Factor	Embryonic	Growth	Mature	Declining
1 Growth rate	Normally much greater than GNP (on small base).	Sustained growth above GNP. New customers. New suppliers. Rate decelerates toward end of stage.	Approximately equals GNP.	Declining demand. Market shrinks as users' needs change.
2 Predictability of growth potential	Hard to define accurately. Small portion of demand being satisfied. Market forecasts differ widely.	Greater percentage of demand is met and upper limits of demand becoming clearer. Discontinuities, such as price reductions based on economies of scale, may occur.	Potential well defined. Competition specialized to satisfy needs of specific segments.	Known and limited.
3 Product line proliferation	Specialized lines to meet needs of early customers.	Rapid expansion.	Proliferation slows or ceases.	Lines narrow as unprofitable products dropped.
4 Number of competitors	Unpredictable.	Reaches maximum. New entrants attracted by growth and high margins. Some consolidation begins toward end of stage.	Entrenched positions established. Further shakeout of marginal competitors.	New entrants unlikely. Competitors continue to decline.
5 Market share distribution	Unstable. Shares react unpredictably to entrepreneurial insights and timing.	Increasing stability. Typically, a few competitors emerging as strong.	Stable with a few companies often controlling much of industry.	Highly concentrated or fragmented as industry segments and/or is localized.
6 Customer stability	Trial usage with little customer loyalty.	Some loyalty. Repeat usage with many seeking alternative suppliers.	Well-developed buying patterns with customer loyalty. Competitors understand purchase dynamics and it is difficult for a new supplier to win over accounts.	Extremely stable. Suppliers dwindle and customers less motivated to seek alternatives.
7 Ease of entry	Normally easy. No one dominates. Customers' expectations uncertain. If barriers exist, they are usually technology, capital, or fear of the unknown.	More difficult. Market franchises and/or economies of scale may exist, yet new business is still available without directly confronting competition.	Difficult. Market leaders established. New business must be "won" from others.	Little or no incentive to enter.
8 Technology	Plays an important role in matching product characteristics to market needs. Frequent product changes.	Product technology vital early, while process technology more important later in this stage.	Process and material substitution focus. Product requirements well known and relatively undemanding. May be a thrust to renew the industry via new technology.	Technological content is known, stable, and accessible.

stand what market share really means is to assume that their company has only a small share of the market. In short, if a company is successful, it probably has a large share of a small market segment. Table 4-1 shows a checklist used by one large company to help it determine the location of its markets in the life cycle.

DIFFUSION OF INNOVATION

An interesting and useful extension of the product life cycle is what is known as *diffusion of innovation*. This concept is also discussed in chapter 5.
Diffusion is:

1 The adoption
2 of new products or services
3 over time
4 by consumers
5 within social systems
6 as encouraged by marketing

Diffusion refers to the cumulative percentage of adopters of a new product or service over time. Everett Rogers examined some of the social forces that explain the product life cycle. The body of knowledge often referred to as *reference theory* (which incorporates work on group norms, group pressures, and other dynamics) helps explain the snowball effect of diffusion. Rogers found that the actual rate of diffusion is a function of the following aspects of a product:

1. Relative advantage (over existing products)
2. Compatibility (with factors such as life-styles and values)
3. Communicability (is it easy to communicate?)
4. Complexity (is it complicated?)
5. Divisibility (can it be tried out on a small scale before commitment?)

Diffusion is also a function of the newness of the product itself, which can be classified broadly in three headings, as follows:

1. Continuous innovation (e.g., the new miracle ingredient)
2. Dynamically continuous innovation (e.g., disposable lighter)
3. Discontinuous (e.g., microwave oven)

However, Rogers found that for all new products, not everyone adopts new products at the same time and that a universal pattern emerges, as shown in Figure 4-4.

In general, innovators think for themselves and try new things (when relevant). Early adopters, who have status in society, are opinion leaders, and they adopt successful products, making them acceptable and respectable. The early majority, who are more conservative and who have slightly above-average status, are more deliberate and only adopt products that have social approbation. The late majority, who have below-average status and are skeptical, adopt products much later than the first three categories. The laggards, with lower status and income and less education than the earlier adopters, see life through the rearview mirror and are the last to adopt products.

This particular piece of research can be very useful, particularly for advertising and personal selling. For example, if you can develop a typology for opinion leaders, you can target your early advertising and sales effort specifically at them. Once the first 7 to 8 percent of opinion leaders have adopted your product, there is a good chance that the early majority will try it. Once 10 to 12 percent is reached, the champagne can be opened, because there is a good chance that the rest will adopt your product.

The general characteristics of opinion leaders are that they are venturesome, socially integrated, cosmopolitan, socially mobile, and privileged. So you need to ask about the specific characteristics of these customers in your particular industry. You can then tailor your advertising and selling message specifically to these customers.

Diffusion of innovation analysis can, however, be both a practical diagnostic and a forecasting tool. Table 4-2 illustrates how forecasts, and eventually strategic marketing plans, were developed from the use of the diffusion of innovation curve for computerized business systems for the

Figure 4-4
Adopter
Categories

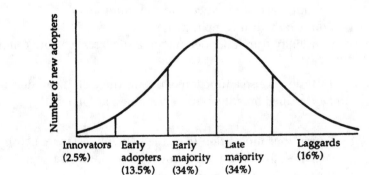

TABLE 4-2 Using Diffusion Theory to Create Sales Objectives

1	Number of contracting firms	160,596
2	Number of firms employing 4–79 direct employees	43,400
3	Exclude painters, plasterers, etc.	6,100
4	Conservative estimate of main target area	37,300 or 23% of total (1)
5	Using the Pareto (80/20 rule) likelihood that 20 percent will be main target area, i.e. 160,596 × 20%	(2) 32,000
6	Total number of firms in construction industry	217,785
7	Number of firms classified by sales from $200,000 to $2,000,000	
	$100–499	26,698
	$500–999	10,651
	$1,000–5,000	5,872
		43,221 (3)

Figure 4-5
Diffusion of Innovation Curves

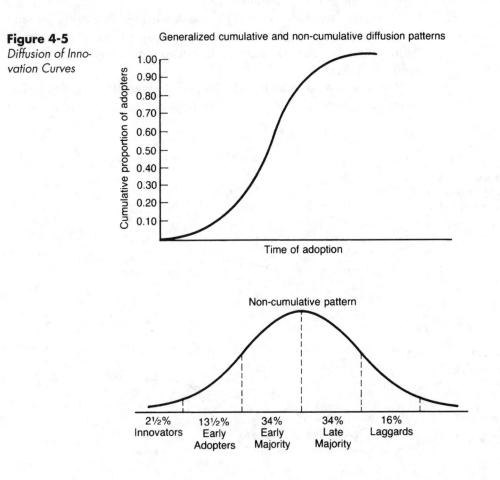

Generalized cumulative and non-cumulative diffusion patterns

construction industry in one market. In the example three independent estimates are made of market size to establish the current position on the diffusion of innovation curve.

The diffusion of innovation curve, in conjunction with the product life cycle, helps to explain the dynamics of markets. Figure 4-5 illustrates this relation. It shows that when all potential users of a product are using it, the market is a replacement market.

PRODUCT PORTFOLIO

We might well imagine that at any point in time, a review of a company's different products would reveal different stages of growth, maturity, and decline. In Figure 4-6, the dotted line represents the time of analysis. This shows one product in severe decline, one product in its introductory stage, and one in the saturation stage.

If the objective is to grow in profitability over a long period of time, analysis of the product portfolio should reveal a situation like the one in Figure 4-7, in which new product introductions are timed to ensure continuous sales growth.

The idea of a portfolio is for a company to meet its objectives by balancing sales growth, cash flow, and risk. As individual products progress

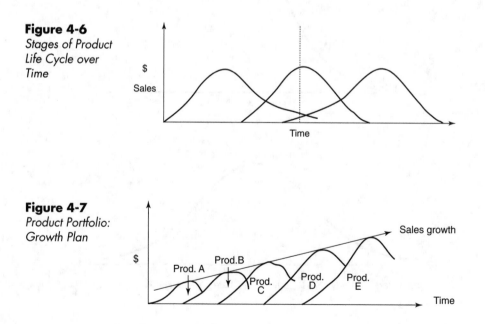

Figure 4-6
Stages of Product Life Cycle over Time

Figure 4-7
Product Portfolio: Growth Plan

or decline and as markets grow or shrink, the overall nature of the company's product portfolio changes. It is therefore essential that the entire portfolio be reviewed regularly and that an active policy toward new product development and divestment of old products be pursued. In this respect, the work of the Boston Consulting Group (BCG), begun in the early 1960s, has had a profound effect on the way managements think about this subject and about their product and market strategy.

UNIT COSTS AND MARKET SHARE

There are two parts to the thinking behind the work of the BCG. One is concerned with *market share*, the other with *market growth*. One becomes better at doing things the more one does them. This phenomenon is known as the *learning curve*. It manifests itself especially with items such as labor efficiency, work specialization, and methods improvement.

Benefits such as process innovations, productivity from plant and equipment, and product design improvements are a part of the *experience effect*. In addition to the experience effect, and not necessarily mutually exclusive, are *economies of scale* that come with growth. For example, capital costs do not increase in direct proportion to capacity, which results in lower depreciation charges per unit of output, lower operating costs in the form of the number of operatives, lower marketing, sales, administration, and research and development costs, and lower raw materials and shipping costs. It is generally recognized, however, that cost decline applies more to the value-added elements of cost than to bought-in supplies. The BCG discovered that costs decline by as much as 30 percent for every doubling of cumulative output and that costs decline forever—that is, every time cumulative output doubles, costs decline by a percentage, the so-called *experience curve* percentage.

The implications of this phenomenon for marketing strategy are quite profound. If this reduction in costs is obtained, the firm with the greater volume is going to have a cost advantage over the firm with smaller volume. With a cost advantage, the firm can be more competitive (with more margin to spend on any or all elements of the marketing mix. Irrespective of what happens to the price of your product, providing you have the greatest volume (and therefore the highest market share) you will always be more profitable and more competitive than your competitors.

This is not to say that there is a casual relation between market share and profitability. The experience effect is not automatic. Simple increases in production or output without working smarter do not lead to declining costs. The experience effect is a reflection of companies in industries that constantly continued to innovate in design, process, and materials to increase their productivity and lower their costs. Integrated circuits and computer memory are two spectacular examples of the experience effect in action.

As a rule, market share *per se* is a desirable goal.

Research has confirmed that market share and profitability are related. However, as discussed in chapter 3, you have to be certain that you have carefully defined your market or segment. This explains why it is apparently possible for many small firms to be profitable in large markets. The reason is that they have a large share of a smaller market segment. This is another reason why understanding market segmentation is the key to successful marketing. Nevertheless the evidence provided by the BCG shows overwhelmingly that these laws apply universally, for consumer, industrial, and service markets.

As for *market growth*, in markets that are growing at a very low rate per annum, it is extremely difficult and expensive to increase market share. This is usually because the market is in the steady state (possibly in the saturation phase of the product life cycle) and is dominated by a few large firms that have probably reached a state of equilibrium that is difficult to upset.

In markets that are experiencing a period of high growth, the most attractive policy is to gain market share by taking a larger proportion of the market growth than your competitors. However, such a policy is expensive in promotional terms. Many companies prefer to sit tight and enjoy rates of growth lower than the market rate. The problem with this approach is that these companies are losing market share, which gives cost advantages (hence margin advantages) to competitors.

Because experience with product life cycles shows that the market growth rate will fall when this stage is reached and the market inevitably becomes price sensitive, the product begins to lose money and you will probably be forced out of the market. This knowledge makes it easier to understand the reasons for the demise of many industries in countries of the world where the Japanese have entered the market.

Typical of this is the motorcycle industry in the United Kingdom, in which the output of the Japanese increased from thousands of units to millions of units during a period of market growth, while the output of the British remained steady during the same period. When the market growth rate started to decline, the inevitable happened: the entire British industry collapsed. The only way to recover from this situation is through differentiation and segmentation. The new British Triumph company has successfully reentered the world motorcycle market with a line of British bikes that appeal to riders looking for something different.

THE BOSTON CONSULTING GROUP MATRIX

The BCG combined the foregoing ideas in the form of a simple matrix, which has profound implications for the firm, especially in regard to *cash flow*. Profits are not always an appropriate indicator of portfolio performance, because they often do not reflect changes in the liquid assets of a company, such as inventories, capital equipment, or receivables, and thus do not indicate the true scope for future development. Cash flow, on the other hand, is a key determinant of a company's ability to develop its product portfolio.

The Boston Consulting Group matrix category labels indicate the prospects for products in each quadrant.

The BCG matrix classifies a firm's products according to cash usage and cash generation along the two dimensions described earlier, that is, relative market share and market growth rate. Market share is used because it is an indicator of the ability of a product to generate cash. Market growth is used because it is an indicator of the product's cash requirements. The measurement of market share used is the product's share *relative* to the firm's largest competitor. This is important because it reflects the degree of dominance enjoyed by the product in the market. For example, if company A has a 20 percent market share and its largest competitor also has a 20 percent market share, this position is usually less favorable than if company A had a 20 percent market share and its largest competitor had only a 10 percent market share. The relative ratios would be 1:1 compared with 2:1. This ratio, or measure of market dominance, is measured along a horizontal axis (Figure 4-8).

The definition of high relative market share is taken to be a ratio of one or greater than one. The cut-off point for high, as opposed to low, market growth is defined according to the prevailing circumstances in the industry, but this is often taken as 10 percent. There is, however, no reason why the dividing line on the vertical axis cannot be zero, or even a negative number. It depends entirely on industry, or segment, growth or decline. Sometimes, in very general markets, gross domestic product (GDP) can be used.

The somewhat picturesque labels attached to each of the four categories of products give some indication of the prospects for products in each quadrant. The *question mark* is a product that has not yet achieved a dominant market position and a high cash flow, or perhaps it once had such a position but has slipped back. Question mark products are high users of cash because they are in a growth market. The *star* is probably a new product that has achieved a high market share and may be self-financing in cash terms. *Cash cows* are leaders in mature markets in which there is little additional growth, but a great deal of stability. These are excellent generators of cash and tend to use little because of the state of the market.

Figure 4-8
The Boston Consulting Group Product Portfolio Matrix

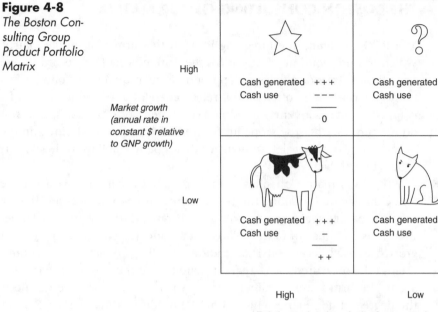

Dogs often have little future and can be a cash drain on the company. They are probably candidates for divestment, although often such products fall into a category aptly described by Peter Drucker as "investments in managerial ego."

The art of product portfolio management becomes a lot clearer. What you are seeking to do is to use the surplus cash generated by the cash cows to invest in stars and to invest in a selected number of question marks (Figure 4-9).

The BCG matrix can be used to forecast the market position of your products, say, five years from now, if you continue to pursue your current policies.

Such a framework also shows the flow of marketing objectives, such as "to achieve 10 percent growth and 20 percent return on investment." Such an objective may be self-defeating. For example, to accept a 10 percent growth rate in a market that is growing at, for example, 15 percent per annum, is likely to prove disastrous in the long run. Likewise, to try to achieve a much higher than market growth rate in a low-growth market is certain to lead to unnecessary price wars and market disruption.

Figure 4-9
*Product Portfolio
Management*

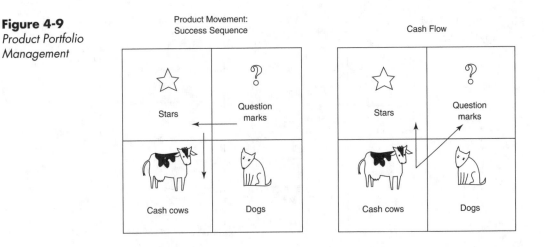

It is also useful to identify the implications of different product and market strategies and new product development policy.

WEAKNESSES IN THE BOSTON CONSULTING GROUP MATRIX APPROACH

Unfortunately, many companies started using the BCG matrix indiscriminately during the 1970s. As a result, it gradually lost its universal appeal. The reason had more to do with lack of real understanding on the part of management than with defects in the method. Nonetheless there are circumstances in which great caution is required in the use of the BCG matrix. Imagine a company with 80 percent of its products in low-growth markets and only 20 percent of its products as market leaders. The matrix would look like the one in Figure 4-10. Almost 65 percent of the company's products are "dogs." To divest these may be tantamount to throwing the baby out with the bath water.

Consider industries in which market share for any single product in the range has little to do with its profitability. Often a low-market-share product enjoys the same production, distribution, and marketing economies of scale as other products in the portfolio, as, for example, in the case of beers and chemical products.

For example, a product manufactured with basically the same components as other large-market-share products is manufactured in the same plant as part of a similar process and is distributed on the same vehicles and through the same outlets. It is easy to see how this low-market-share product can indeed be extremely profitable.

Figure 4-10
*A Doggy Product
Portfolio*

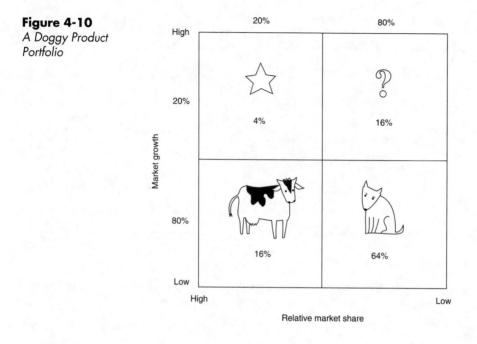

None of this, however, invalidates the work of the BCG, the principles of which can be applied to companies, divisions, subsidiaries, strategic business units, product groups, and products. If great care is taken with the market share axis, the BCG matrix is an extremely valuable planning tool.

DEVELOPMENTS OF THE BCG MATRIX

Complications such as those outlined earlier make the BCG matrix irrelevant in certain situations. Although it is impossible to give absolute rules about what these situations are, businesses should adhere to the following two principles. A business should define its markets in such a way that it can ensure that its costs for key activities are competitive and in such a way that it can develop specialized skills in servicing those markets and overcome a relative cost disadvantage. Both ways of defining itself have to be related to a company's *distinctive competence.*

The BCG approach is fairly criticized as relying on two single factors, that is, relative market share and market growth. To overcome this limitation, and to provide a more flexible approach, General Electric and McKinsey jointly developed a multifactor approach using the same fundamental ideas as the BCG. They used *industry attractiveness* and *business strengths* as the two main axes and built on these dimensions from a number of variables. With these variables and a scheme for weighting them according to their importance, products (or businesses) are classified into one of nine cells in a three-by-three matrix. The same purpose is served as in the BCG matrix (i.e., comparing investment opportunities among products or businesses) but with the difference that multiple criteria are used. These criteria vary according to circumstances but often include those shown in Figure 4-11.

It is not necessary to use a nine-box matrix, and many managers prefer to use a four-box matrix similar to the BCG box. This is our preferred method, because it seems to be more easily understood by and useful to managers.

The four-box directional policy matrix is shown in Figure 4-12. The circles represent sales into an industry, market, or segment. In the same way as in the BCG matrix, each is proportional to that contribution of the segment to sales.

Figure 4-11

The General Electric McKinsey Matrix

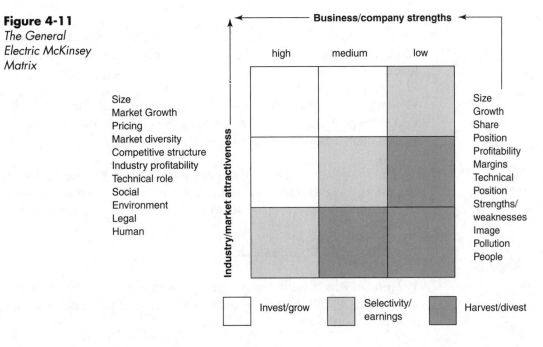

Figure 4-12
*Directional Policy
Matrix*

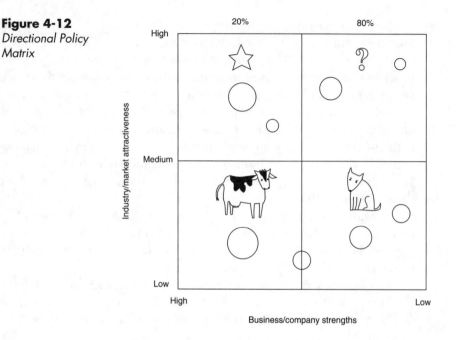

Rather than only two variables, the criteria used for each axis are totally relevant and specific to the company using the matrix. It shows the following:

- Markets categorized on a scale of attractiveness to the firm
- The relative strengths of the firm in each of these markets
- The relative importance of each market

The specific criteria for determining attractiveness are decided by key executives using the matrix. It is advisable to use no more than five or six factors; otherwise the exercise becomes too complex and loses its focus.

The Strategic Business Unit

The level at which a firm can be analyzed with use of the directional policy matrix (DPM) is that of the *strategic business unit* (SBU). The most common definition of an SBU is as follows:

- It has common segments and competitors for most of the products.
- It is a competitor in an external market.
- It is a discrete, separate, and identifiable entity.
- Its manager has control over most of the areas critical to success.

What Is Plotted on the Matrix?

This step is simple to deal with, but confusion can arise because the options are rarely spelled out. Let us take a hypothetical two-dimensional market into which a number of products are sold (Figure 4-13). Each square might be considered a segment, and various combinations can be considered to be the market, as follows:

a. The actual product-customer cells served
b. The intersection of product functions A, B, C and customer groups 2, 3, 4
c. Product functions A, B, C for *all* customer groups
d. Customer groups 2, 3, 4 for *all* product functions
e. The entire matrix

The DPM is useful when there is more than one (at least three and a maximum of ten are suggested) market or segment between which the

Figure 4-13
Factors that Contribute to Market Attractiveness

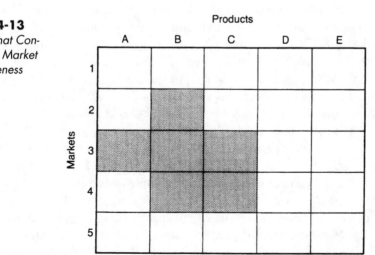

Preparation

Before analysis is begun, the following preparation is recommended:

- Ensure that product profiles are available for all products or services to be scored.
- Define the markets in which the products or services compete.
- Define the time period being scored. Three years is recommended.

- Define the competitors against which the products or services are to be scored.
- Ensure sufficient data are available to score the factors (when no data are available, this is not a problem as long as a sensible approximation can be made for the factors).
- Ensure up-to-date sales forecasts are available for all products or services, including any new products or services.

planner wishes to distinguish. These can be either existing or potential markets, in which a market is defined as follows:

> An identifiable group of customers with requirements in common that are, or may become, *significant* in determining a separate strategy.

A market in this sense is clearly a matter of management judgment. At the beginning of any exercise using the DPM, the priority must be to define correctly the unit of analysis in terms of the combinations of product and markets. For example, it is clearly possible to put 25 circles (or crosses, where there are no sales) on a portfolio matrix with markets 1 through 5 on the vertical axis and each of products A through E on the horizontal axis (i.e., choice e, listed earlier), but that would result in a confusing array of circles and crosses.

It would also be possible to put six circles on a matrix. That is, the actual product-customer cells served (choice a), with markets 2, 3, and 4 on the vertical axis and products A, B, and C as appropriate for each of these served markets on the horizontal axis.

An alternative to individual plotting of products A, B, and C is to plot an aggregate value or volume for all products in any served market. Any of the combinations listed in the example above also could be used. The user has to decide early exactly what will be the unit of analysis for the purpose of determining the size of each circle that appears in the matrix.

To summarize, the principal unit of analysis for the purpose of entering data is the user's definition of *product for market*.

Ten Steps to Producing the Directional Policy Matrix

1. Define the products or services for markets that are to be used during the analysis.
2. Define the criteria for market attractiveness.
3. Score the relevant products or services for the market.
4. Define the organization's relative strengths for each product or service for market.
5. Analyze and draw conclusions from the relative position of each product or service for market.
6. Draw conclusions from the analysis with a view to generating objectives and strategies.
7. Position the circles on the box assuming no change to current policies. That is, a *forecast* is made of the future position of the circles. This step is optional.
8. Redraw the portfolio to position the circles where the organization wants them to be. These are the *objectives* the organization wants to achieve for each product or service for market.
9. Detail the strategies to be implemented to achieve the objectives.
10. Detail the appropriate financial consequences in terms of growth rate by product or service for market and return on sales.

Analysis Team

To improve the quality of scoring, it is recommended that a group of people from a number of different functions score. This encourages the challenging of traditional views by means of discussion. We recommend that no more than six people be involved in the analysis.

TWO KEY DEFINITIONS

Market attractiveness is a measure of the *potential* of the marketplace to yield growth in sales and profits. It is important to emphasize that assessment of market attractiveness is objective, made with data *external* to the organization. The criteria themselves are determined by the organization performing the exercise and are relevant to the objectives the organization is trying to achieve, but are independent of the position of the organization in its markets.

Business strength and position is a measure of an organization's *actual* strengths in the marketplace (i.e., the degree to which it can take advantage of a market opportunity). It is an objective assessment of an organization's ability to satisfy market needs relative to competitors' ability to satisfy needs.

THE PROCESS

Step 1: List the Population of Products or Services for Markets That You Intend to Include in the Matrix

The list can consist of countries, companies, subsidiaries, regions, products, markets, segments, customers, distributors, or any other unit of analysis that is important. The DPM can be used at any level in an organization and for any kind of SBU.

Step 2: Define Market Attractiveness Factors

In this step, list the factors you want to consider in comparing the attractiveness of your markets. It is important to list the markets in which you intend to apply the criteria before deciding on the criteria themselves, since the purpose of the vertical axis is to discriminate between more and less attractive markets. The criteria themselves must be specific to the population and must not be changed for different markets in the same population. This is a combination of a number of factors. These factors, however, can usually be summarized under the following three headings (Table 4-3):

Growth rate Average annual growth rate of revenue spent by that segment (percentage growth 1995 over 1996, *plus* percentage growth 1996 over 1997, *plus* percentage growth 1998 over 1999, divided by 3). If preferred, compound average growth rate can be used.

Accessible Market Size An attractive market not only is large but also can be accessed. One way of calculating ability to access a market is to es-

TABLE 4-3 Classification of Market Attractiveness Factors

Factors	Example Weight
Growth rate	40
Accessible market size	20
Profit potential	40
Total	100

Note: Because profit equals market size multiplied by margin multiplied by growth, it would be reasonable to expect the *weighting* against each of these to be at *least* as shown, although an even higher weight on *growth* would be understandable in some circumstances (in which case, the corresponding weight for the others is reduced).

TABLE 4-4   Profit Potential Estimate: Porter's Five Forces

Subfactor	10 = Low 1 = High	× Weight	Weighted Factor Score
1 Intensity of competition	10	50	500
2 Threat of substitute	8	5	40
3 Threat of new entrants	7	5	35
4 Power of suppliers	9	10	90
5 Power of customer	6	30	180
Profit potential factor score	40	100	845

timate the *total* revenue of the segment in *t* + 3, *less* revenue impossible to access, regardless of investment made. Another method is to use total market size. This method does not involve any managerial judgment, which can distort the truth. *The second is the preferred and more frequently used method.* A market size factor score is simply the score multiplied by the weight (20 in the example).

Profit Potential This is much more difficult to deal with and varies considerably from industry to industry. For example, Porter's Five Forces model can be used to estimate the profit potential of a segment, as in the example in Table 4-4. In this example, the total score is 845.

If each of the forces is scored at 10, which is low, the total score is 1,000 in contrast to a score of 100 if each force is scored at the high level of 1. In other words, low competitive intensity, a low threat of substitutes and new entrants, and low power of suppliers and customers produce the highest score for profit potential.

An alternative is to use a combination of these and industry-specific factors. In the case of the pharmaceutical industry, the factors may be as in Table 4-5.

These are clearly a proxy for profit potential. Each is weighted according to its importance. The weights add to 100 to give a *profit potential factor score*, as in the Porter's Five Forces example cited earlier. After this calculation, the profit potential factor score is simply multiplied by the weight (40 in the example).

Variations

Naturally, growth, size, and profit do not encapsulate the requirements of all organizations. For example, in the case of an orchestra, artistic satisfaction may be an important consideration. In another case, social

TABLE 4-5 Profit Potential Estimate: Industry-Specific Factors

Subfactor	High	Medium	Low	× Weight	Weighted Factor Score
1 Unmet medical needs (efficacy)				30	
2 Unmet medical needs (safety)				25	
3 Unmet medical needs (convenience)				15	
4 Price potential				10	
5 Competitive intensity				10	
6 Cost of market entry				10	
Profit potential factor score					

considerations may be important. In yet another, cyclicity may be a factor. It is possible, then, to add another heading, such as *Risk* or *Other* to the three factors listed at the beginning of step 2. In general, however, it is possible to reduce the list to the three main headings with subfactors incorporated into them.

Step 3: Score the Relevant Products or Services for Markets

In this step you should score the products or services for markets against the factors defined in step 1. One question that frequently arises is, can market attractiveness factors change while the DPM is being constructed? The answer to this is, no. Once agreed, under no circumstances should market attractiveness factors be changed; otherwise the attractiveness of the markets is not being evaluated against common criteria, and the matrix becomes meaningless. Scores, however, are specific to each market.

Another question is, can the circles move vertically? *No* is the obvious answer, although *yes* is possible if the matrix shows the current level of attractiveness at the present time. This implies performing one set of calculations for the present according to market attractiveness factors to locate markets on the vertical axis, then performing another set of calculations for a future period (for example, three years' time) on the basis of forecasts made with the same factors. In practice, it is easier to carry out only the latter calculation, in which case the circles can move only horizontally.

Step 4: Define Business Strengths and Position Analysis Organization Level

This is a measure of the *actual* strengths of an organization in the marketplace and differs according to market or segment opportunity. The factors that determine the strengths of an organization usually are a combination of an organization's relative strengths in relation to competitors' strengths in connection with *customer-facing needs,* that is, things required by the customer. These can often be summarized as follows:

- Product requirements
- Price requirements
- Service requirements
- Promotion requirements

The weight given to each requirement should be specific to each market or segment. In the same way that *profit* on the market attractiveness axis can be broken down into subheadings, each type of requirement can be broken down and analyzed. This process is strongly recommended. These subfactors should be dealt with in the same way as the subfactors described for market attractiveness. For example, in the case of pharmaceuticals, product strengths can be represented as follows:

- Relative product strengths
- Relative product safety
- Relative product convenience
- Relative cost effectiveness

Broadening the Analysis

An organization's relative strengths in meeting customer-facing needs is a function of its *capabilities* in connection with *industry-wide success factors.* For example, if a depot is necessary in each large town or city for any organization to succeed in an industry and the organization performing the analysis does not have a depot, it is likely that this deficiency accounts for poor performance in the category of customer service, which is a customer requirement. If it is necessary to have low feedstock costs for any organization to succeed in an industry and the organization conducting the analysis does not have this criterion, it is likely that this deficiency accounts for poor performance in the category of price, which is a customer requirement.

In the same way that subfactors should be estimated to arrive at market attractiveness factors, an assessment of the capabilities of an organization in respect to *industry-wide success factors* can be made to understand what needs to be done in the organization to satisfy customer needs. This assessment is separate from quantification of the business strengths and position axis. The purpose is to translate the analysis into actionable propositions for other functions within the organization, such as purchasing, production, and distribution.

In the case of pharmaceuticals, for example, factors such as patent life are simply an indication of the capability of an organization to provide product differentiation. They are irrelevant to the physician but have to be taken into account by the organization conducting the analysis.

How to Deal with Business Strengths and Position

The first concern is quantification of business strengths within a market. The only way a company can do this is to understand the real needs and wants of the chosen customer group, find out by means of market research how well these needs are being met by existing products in the market, and seek to satisfy these needs better than their competitors.

The following is a typical calculation to assess the strength of a company in a market. The information was gathered by means of a self-assessment questionnaire. The following three questions were used to plot the firm's (SBU's) position on the horizontal axis (competitive position and business strengths):

What are the key things that any competitor has to do right to succeed (i.e., what are the critical success factors in this industry sector)?

How important is each of these critical success factors (measured comparatively on a scale of 1 to 100)?

How do you and each of your competitors score (out of 10) on each of the critical success factors?

These questions yield the information necessary to make an overall assessment of the competitive strengths of an SBU (Table 4-6).

The analysis shows the following:

- This organization is not the market leader
- All competitors score more than 5.0

TABLE 4-6 Competitive Strength: Overall Estimate

Critical Success Factors (What Are the Key Things That a Company Must Do Right to Succeed?)	Weighting (How Important Is Each of These CSFs? Score out of 100.)		Strengths/Weaknesses Analysis (Score Yourself and Each of Your Main Competitors out of 10 on Each of the CSFs, Then Multiply the Score by the Weight.)			
				Competition		
			You	Comp A	Comp B	Comp C
1 Product	20		9 = 1.8	6 = 1.2	5 = 1.0	4 = 0.8
2 Price	10		8 = 0.8	5 = 0.5	6 = 0.6	10 = 0.1
3 Service	50		5 = 2.5	9 = 4.5	7 = 3.5	6 = 3.0
4 Image	20		8 = 1.6	8 = 1.6	5 = 1.0	3 = 0.6
These should normally be viewed from the customer's point of view.	**Total 100**	**Total score × weight**	**6.7**	**7.8**	**6.1**	**5.4**

The problem with this and many similar calculations is that rarely does this method allow one to discriminate sufficiently well to indicate the relative strengths of a number of products in a particular company's product or market portfolio. Many of the SBU's products would appear on the left of the matrix.

A method is needed to prevent all products from appearing on the left of the matrix. This can be achieved by use of a ratio, as in the BCG matrix. This indicates a company's position relative to the best in the market.

In the example provided, competitor A has the most strengths in the market, so your organization needs to make some improvements. To reflect this, your weighted score should be compared with that of competitor A (the highest weighted score). Thus 6.7 : 7.8 = 0.86 : 1.

If we were to plot this on a logarithmic scale on the horizontal axis, this would place our organization to the right of the dividing line as follows:

3×		0.3

(Make the left-hand extreme point 3× and start the scale on the right at 0.3). A scale of 3× to 0.3 was chosen because such a band is likely to encapsulate most extremes of competitive advantage. If it does not, simply change it to suit your own circumstances.

Step 5: Producing the Directional Policy Matrix

Circles are drawn on a four-box matrix. Market size (as defined in step 2) is used to determine the area of the circle. An organization's market share can be put in as a wedge in each circle. An organization's own sales in each market also can be used. It is advisable to use both variables and compare them to see how closely actual sales match the opportunities.

Step 6: Analysis and Generation of Marketing Objectives and Strategies

The objective of producing a DPM is to see the portfolio of products or services for markets relative to each other in the context of the criteria used. This analysis indicates whether the portfolio is well balanced and should give a clear indication of any problems. As an option, it is sometimes advisable to move to step 7 at this point.

Step 7: Forecasting (Optional)

The forecast position of the circles is made by means of rescoring the products or services for markets in three years' time, if the organization does not change its strategies (see step 3). This forecast indicates whether the position is becoming worse or better. It is not absolutely necessary to change the scores on the vertical axis (see step 3).

Step 8: Setting Marketing Objectives

Setting marketing objectives involves changing the volumes and values or market share (marketing objectives) and the scores on the horizontal axis (relative strength in market) to achieve the desired volumes and values. Conceptually, one is picking up the circle and moving and revising it without specifying how this is to be achieved. Strategies are then defined, which involve words and changes to individual critical success factor scores (see step 9).

Step 9: Detail Strategies

Detailing of strategies involves making specific statements about the marketing strategies to be used to achieve the desired volumes and values.

Step 10: Sales and Profit Forecasts

Sales and profit forecasts are made as follows (Figure 4-14):

1. Plot average percentage growth in sales revenue by segment ($t - 3$ to $t0$)

   Plot average percentage return on sales (ROS) by segment ($t - 3$ to $t0$)

2. Plot *forecast* average percentage growth in sales revenue by segment ($t0$ to $t + 3$)

   Plot *forecast* average percentage ROS by segment ($t0$ to $t + 3$)

A large chemical company used the DPM to select fifty distributors from the 450 with whom they were dealing. They needed to do this because the market was in decline and the distributors had begun *buying* for customers rather than *selling* for the supplier. This led to a dramatic fall in prices. The only way the chemical company could begin to tackle the problem was by appointing a number of exclusive distributorships. The issue of which distributorships to choose was tackled by use of the DPM, because some distributorships clearly were more attractive than others, and the company had varying strengths in its dealings with each distributor.

Figure 4-14
Sales and Profit Forecasts Versus Historic Perfor-mance

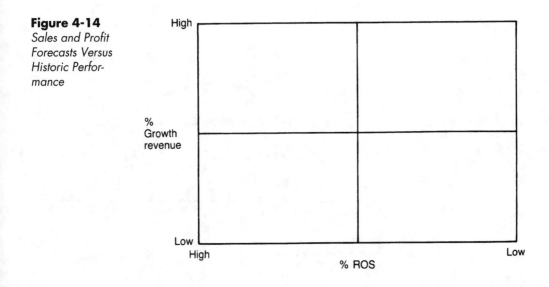

COMBINING PRODUCT LIFE CYCLES AND PORTFOLIO MANAGEMENT

Figure 4-15 illustrates the consequences of failing to appreciate the implications of the product life cycle concept and the combination of market share and market growth.

Companies A and B both start out with question marks (wildcats) in years 5 and 6 in a growing market. Company A invests in building market share and quickly turns into a star. Company B, meanwhile, manages its products for profit over a four-year period so that while still growing it steadily loses market share (i.e., it remains a question mark or wildcat). In year 10, when the market becomes saturated (when typically competitive pressures intensify), company B with its low market share (hence typically higher costs and lower margins) cannot compete and quickly drops out of the market. Company A, on the other hand, aggressively defends its market share and goes on to enjoy a period of approximately ten years with a product that has become a cash cow. Company B, by pursuing a policy of short-term profit maximization, loses at least ten years of profit potential.

The analyses described in this chapter should be an integral part of the marketing audit. The audit should contain a product life cycle for each major product, and an attempt should be made (using other audit information) to predict the future shape of the life cycle. It should also contain a product portfolio matrix that shows the present position of the products.

Figure 4-15
Short-term Profit Maximization Versus Market Share and Long-term Profit Maximization

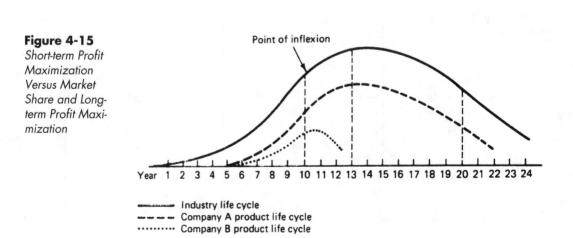

━━━━ Industry life cycle
━ ━ ━ Company A product life cycle
•••••••• Company B product life cycle

QUESTIONS SUCCESSFUL COMPANIES ASK

1. Do we need to strengthen our brand name?
2. What is our market share? Are we holding, gaining, or losing share?
3. Should we get rid of our "dogs"? (This decision is always a matter of timing. It is possible sometimes to squeeze extra earnings from a "dog." Sometimes a "dog" is supportive of another product. Sometimes a "dog" can be profitable because it shares in the economies of scale of another product in the range.)
4. What unique value do we create for our customers?

5 Marketing Objectives and Strategies

Chapter 5 defines marketing objectives and how they relate to corporate objectives and shows how to set them. Where and how to start the process of marketing planning by means of gap analysis is described, and new product development is discussed as a growth strategy. Finally, the definition and formulation of marketing strategies are explained. Setting objectives and formulating strategies are the key steps in the marketing planning process. Realistic and achievable objectives must be set for a company's major products in each of its major markets. Unless this step is performed well, everything that follows will lack focus and cohesion. It is a question of deciding on the right target. There is no gain in scoring a bull's-eye on the wrong target. Once the correct objectives are identified, strategies to achieve these objectives must be formulated.

Once again, the actual contents of a strategic marketing plan are described in chapter 12. It is important, however, to read chapter 5 carefully before trying to complete the crucial step of defining marketing objectives and strategies.

MARKETING OBJECTIVES: WHAT THEY ARE AND HOW THEY RELATE TO CORPORATE OBJECTIVES

Setting objectives is an essential step in the planning process. A company that has set an objective knows what it expects to accomplish with its strategies and when a particular strategy has worked. Without objectives, strategy decisions and all that follows take place in a vacuum.

The logical approach to setting objectives is to proceed from the broad to the specific.

Most experts agree that the logical approach to the difficult task of setting marketing objectives is to proceed from the broad to the specific. The starting point is a statement of the nature of the business (the mission statement), from which flows the broad company objectives. The broad company objectives must be translated into key result areas, which are the areas in which success is vital to the firm. Market penetration and growth rate of sales are examples of key result areas. The third step is the establishment of sub-objectives necessary to accomplish the broad objectives, such as product sales volume goals, geographic expansion, product

Figure 5-1 *Hierarchy of Objectives and Strategies*

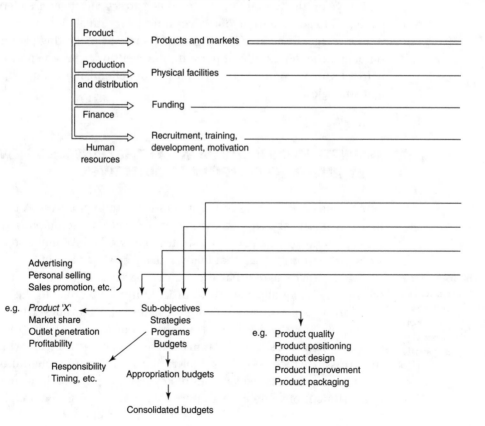

**Marketing planning in a
corporate framework**

Corporate mission
Define the business and its boundaries
using considerations such as:
- distinctive competence
- aspirations
- environmental trends
- resource market trends
- stakeholder expectations

Corporate objectives
e.g. ROI, ROS, image, social responsibility, etc.

Corporate strategies
e.g. involve corporate resources, and must be within corporate business boundaries

Product → Products and markets

Production
and distribution → Physical facilities

Finance → Funding

Human
resources → Recruitment, training,
development, motivation

Advertising
Personal selling
Sales promotion, etc. }

e.g. *Product 'X'* ← Sub-objectives
Market share   Strategies
Outlet penetration   Programs   e.g. Product quality
Profitability   Budgets   Product positioning
                              Product design
Responsibility   Product Improvement
Timing, etc.   Appropriation budgets   Product packaging

Consolidated budgets

Figure 5-1 *Hierarchy of Objectives and Strategies* (Continued)

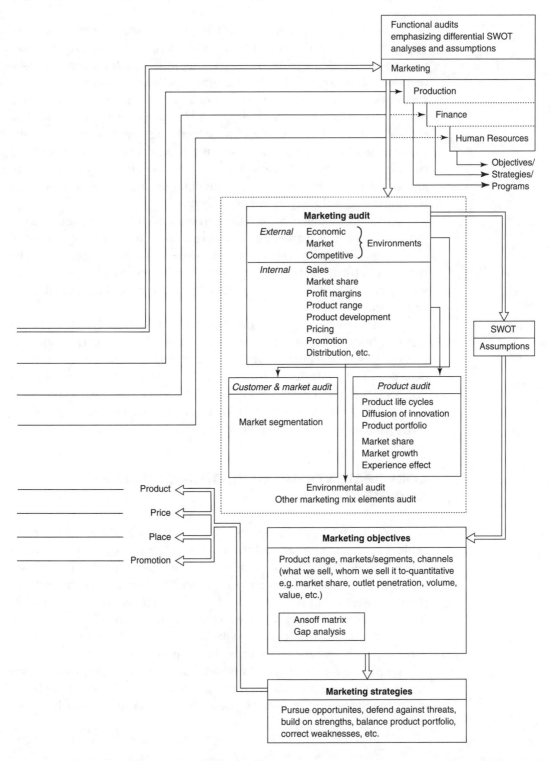

line extension, and specific objectives for each element of the marketing mix.

Advertising objectives, for example, must be wholly consistent with wider objectives. Objectives set in this way integrate the advertising effort with the other elements in the marketing mix, which ensures a consistent, logical marketing plan. For example, the buying process begins with awareness, and creating awareness is one of the functions of advertising. An objective of attaining, for example, 107 unaided awareness recalls in a specific market is an example of an advertising objective that might be part of a marketing plan. The result of this process is objectives that are consistent with the strategic plan, attainable within budget limitations, and compatible with the strengths, limitations, and economics of other functions within the organization.

Marketing strategies within the corporate plan become operating objectives within the marketing department, and strategies at the general level within the marketing department become operating objectives at the next level down, so that an intricate web of interrelated objectives and strategies is built up at all levels within the framework of the overall company plan.

A hierarchy of objectives and strategies can be traced back to the initial corporate objectives. Figure 5-1 illustrates this point. The most important point, however, apart from clarifying the difference between objectives and strategies, is that the farther down the hierarchical chain one goes, the less likely it is that a stated objective will make a cost-effective contribution to company profits, unless it derives logically and directly from an objective at a higher level.

CORPORATE VERSUS MARKETING OBJECTIVES AND STRATEGIES

A business starts with resources and wants to use those resources to achieve something. What the business wants to achieve is a *corporate objective*, which describes a desired destination or result. How objectives are achieved is a *strategy*. Frequently the objective is expressed in terms of profit, because profit is the means of satisfying shareholders and because it is the one universally accepted criterion by which efficiency can be evaluated. Objectives are also frequently expressed in terms of sales or revenue, since revenue is what sustains employment and jobs.

Specific targets, such as expanding market share, creating a new image, and achieving a certain percentage increase in sales are strategies at the corporate level. They are the means by which a company achieves its profit objectives or its sales or revenue objectives. However, for a subunit of a company that is responsible for, say, increasing the company's share of a specific market, increasing market share is a goal. Thus what is a corporate strategy becomes a divisional goal. How the division reaches the goal of increasing market share for its products is a strategy.

HOW TO SET MARKETING OBJECTIVES

Marketing objectives are about products and markets only.

The Ansoff matrix is a useful tool for setting marketing objectives.

A firm's competitive situation can be simplified to two dimensions only—products and markets. To put it even more simply, Ansoff's framework is about what is sold (the product) and to whom it is sold (the market). Within this framework Ansoff identifies the following four possible courses of action for the firm:

- Selling existing products to existing markets
- Extending existing products to new markets
- Developing new products for existing markets
- Developing new products for new markets

The matrix in Figure 5-2 depicts these concepts.

It is clear that the range of possible marketing objectives is wide, because there are degrees of technological newness and degrees of market newness. Ansoff's matrix provides a logical framework in which marketing objectives can be developed under each of the four main headings.

Figure 5-2
Ansoff Matrix

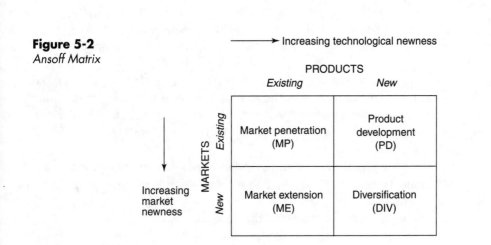

83

Marketing objectives are about products and markets only. Because it is only by obtaining sales that a company's financial goals can be achieved, elements such as advertising, pricing, and service levels are the means (or strategies) to do this. Factors such as pricing objectives, sales promotion objectives, and advertising objectives should not be confused with marketing objectives.

Marketing objectives are selected qualitative and quantitative commitments, usually stated either in standards of performance for a given operating period or conditions to be achieved by given dates. *Performance standards* are usually stated in terms of sales volume and various measures of profitability. *Conditions* to be attained are usually a percentage of market share and various other commitments, such as a percentage of the total number of a given type of retail outlet.

Objectives must be specific enough to guide an organization to the action required, and they must be the yardstick with which performance is measured. Objectives are the core of managerial action; they provide direction to the plans. By asking where the operation should be at some future date, a company determines objectives. Vague objectives are counterproductive to sensible planning. They are usually the result of the human propensity for wishful thinking, which often seems more like cheerleading than serious marketing leadership.

It is arguable whether directional terms such as "decrease," "optimize," and "minimize" should be used as objectives. Unless there is a means of measurement, a yardstick, with which to quantify movement toward achieving an objective, setting objectives does not serve any useful purpose.

A marketing objective contains three important elements. An objective contains the following three elements:

1. The particular attribute that is chosen as a measure of efficiency
2. The yardstick or scale with which the attribute is measured
3. The particular value on the scale that the firm seeks to attain

For example, in the objective of number one share of global market position, share of market is the attribute, the world market is the scale, and number one rank is the value. Marketing objectives are about each of the four main categories of the Ansoff matrix, as follows:

1. Existing products in existing markets. These are many and varied and must be set for all existing major products and customer groups (segments).
2. New products in existing markets

3. Existing products in new markets
4. New products in new markets

Simply defined, product and market strategy means the route chosen to achieve company goals through the range of products it offers to its chosen market segments. Product and market strategy represents a commitment to a future direction for the firm. Marketing objectives are concerned solely with products and markets.

The general marketing directions that lead to the objective flow from the life cycle and portfolio analysis conducted in the audit and revolve around the following logical decisions:

1. *Maintain* usually refers to the "cash cow" type of product and market and reflects the desire to maintain competitive positions.
2. *Improve* usually refers to the "star" type of products and markets and reflects the desire to improve the competitive position in attractive markets.
3. *Harvest* usually refers to the "dog" type of product and market and reflects the desire to relinquish competitive position in favor of short-term profit and cash flow.
4. *Exit* usually refers to the "dog" type of product and market and sometimes the "question mark." It reflects a desire to divest because of a weak competitive position or because the cost of staying in the market is prohibitive and the risk associated with improving position too high.
5. *Enter* usually refers to a new business area.

Great care should be taken not to follow slavishly any set of "rules" or guidelines related to the foregoing decisions. The use of labels such as *dog* and *cash cow* should be avoided as a reference to actual businesses or products.

A full list of marketing guidelines as a precursor to establishment of objectives is given in Table 5-1. Figure 5-3 includes guidelines for functions other than marketing. A warning is that such general guidelines not be followed blindly. They are included as checklists of questions that should be asked about each major product in each major market before marketing objectives and strategies are set.

It is at this stage that the circles in the directional policy matrix (DPM) can be moved to show their relative size and position in three years. You can do this to show first where the circles will be if the company takes no action and second where you want them to be. The latter positions will

TABLE 5-1 Strategies Suggested by Portfolio Matrix Analysis

	Business strengths	
	High	**Low**
High	*Invest for growth* Defend leadership, gain if possible Accept moderate short-term profits and negative cash flow Consider geographic expansion, product line expansion, product differentiation Upgrade production introduction effort Aggressive marketing posture, viz. selling, advertising, pricing, sales promotion service levels, as appropriate	*Opportunistic* The options are: (i) Move it to the left if resources are available to invest in it (ii) Keep a low profile until funds are available (iii) Divest to a buyer able to exploit the opportunity

10 ───

Market attractiveness

	High		**Low**
Low	*Maintain market position, manage for sustained earnings* Maintain market position in most successful product lines Prune less successful product lines Differentiate products to maintain share of key segments Limit discretionary marketing expenditure Stabilize prices, except where a temporary aggressive stance is necessary to maintain market share	*Selective** Acknowledge low growth Do not view as a "marketing" problem Identify and exploit growth segments Emphasize product quality to avoid "commodity" competition Systematically improve productivity Assign talented managers	*Manage for profit* Prune product line aggressively Maximize cash flow Minimize marketing expenditure Maintain or raise prices at the expense of volume

0 ───

| 3.0 | 1.0 | 0.3 |

*Selective refers to those products or markets that fall on or near the vertical dividing line in a directional policy matrix.

become the marketing objectives. Precisely how this task is done is described in chapter 12. It is, however, the key stage in the marketing planning process.

COMPETITIVE STRATEGIES

At this stage of planning, it is helpful to analyze recent developments in competitive strategies. Competitive offerings will always affect how customers perceive the value of your offer. One of the principal purposes of

Figure 5-3 *Program Guidelines Suggested for Different Positioning on the Directional Policy Matrix*

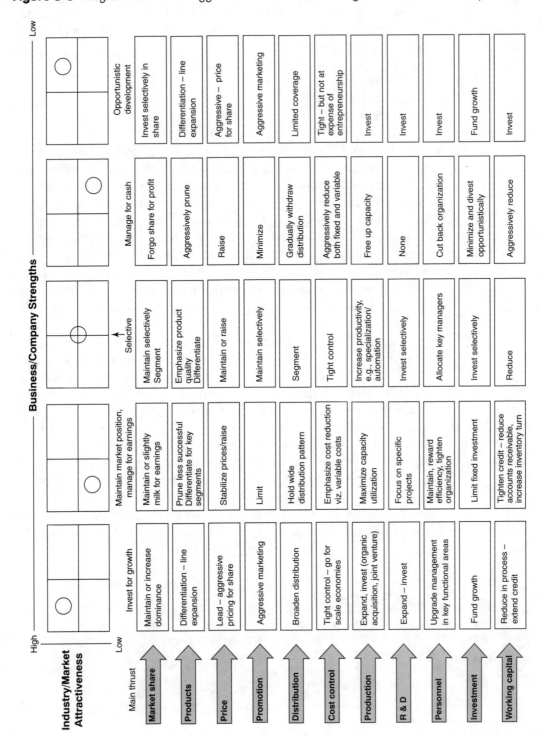

marketing strategy is for you to be able to choose the customers, and hence the markets, with whom you want to deal. In this respect the DPM discussed in chapter 4 is particularly useful. The main components of the strategy are as follows:

- The company
- Customers
- Competitors

So far we have said little about customers, although it is clear that if you are to succeed, you need to work hard at developing a sustainable competitive advantage by creating a unique value for your customers. One contemporary strategy guru has argued that there is no such thing as a sustainable advantage and that in fact all competitive advantages are temporary. In his view, the only way to succeed is to develop a series of temporary advantages (D'Aveni, Richard A., with Robert Gunther. *Hyper-competition.* New York: The Free Press, 1994). D'Aveni has a point. There is certainly no such thing as a strategy that will succeed forever; all strategies must be refreshed and renewed to respond to market and competitor changes.

Michael Porter identified four strategy alternatives (Figure 5-4). Box 1 represents a sound strategy, particularly in commodity-type markets such as bulk chemicals, in which differentiation is difficult to achieve because the chemical composition of the products is identical. In such cases, it is wise to recognize the reality and pursue a productivity drive with the aim of becoming the lowest-cost producer. It is here that the experience effect described in chapter 4 becomes especially important.

Many companies, however, such as Jaguar and BMW, cannot hope to be low-cost producers. As a consequence, their corporate philosophies are geared to differentiation and added value. This represents a sensible strategy for any company that cannot hope to be a world cost beater. Many of the world's great companies succeed by means of such a focus. Many of

Procter & Gamble, the world's premier marketing organization, has announced that it is reducing marketing expenditures to lower prices and reduce the gap between the prices of branded (Procter & Gamble brands) and private label and store brands. P & G is clearly not asleep at the wheel—private label and store brands are increasing market share because of their price advantage. By reducing marketing expenditure, P & G will reduce its costs and be in a position to lower prices, reducing the private label competitive price advantage.

Figure 5-4

Generic Strategy Alternatives

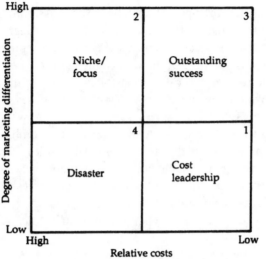

these companies also succeed in pushing themselves into box 3, the outstanding success box, by occupying what can be called "global fortresses." Companies like IBM, Coke, McDonald's, and General Electric typify box 3, in which low costs, differentiation, and world leadership are combined in their corporate strategies.

Box 2, high differentiation and relatively high cost, can be successful as long as the differentiation remains strong and valuable in the customer's mind. This is the strategy for the so-called luxury brands. The key to the success of luxury brands is differentiation, and the key to differentiation is limited production and availability. The success of the Swiss with luxury watches is based on their understanding of this market segment. If there are too many Swiss luxury watches, no matter how good they are, they will lose their differentiation and therefore their value.

Other products have differentiation in their feature set. For example, Apple Computer had ease of use. The threat to Apple has been the introduction of Microsoft Windows 95, which has substantially closed the ease-of-use gap and therefore Apple's differentiation. The Apple strategy is a brilliant example of the disaster ahead for companies that refuse to or do not understand the discipline of market planning. Although it was news to Apple's board of directors, who are at the top of the list of incompetent boards in the annals of world business, the Apple crisis of late 1995 and early 1996 was predictable and avoidable.

What Apple should have recognized is that the company needed to move from box 2 to box 3 to continue to succeed. To do that, the company needed to lower the cost of Apple systems, and to do that they needed to recognize that Apple would have to aggressively license its operating system to manufacturers of personal computers. If Apple had done the obvious, it would be a major challenger to or perhaps the leader in the operating system world market for personal computers. In other words, Apple would have been the Microsoft of the world, not a company in perpetual crisis.

Only box 4 remains. Box 4 shows that a combination of commodity-type markets and high relative costs will result in disaster sooner or later. A position here is tenable only while demand exceeds supply. When these markets mature, there is little hope for companies that find themselves in this unenviable position. What Apple did was move from box 2 to box 4—from niche to disaster—when a competitor (Microsoft) took the ease-of-use advantage.

An important point to remember when thinking about differentiation as a strategy is that your plan must be cost effective. It is a myth that sloppy management and high costs are acceptable as long as the product has a good image and lots of added value. When you think about differentiation, refer to the section on benefit analysis in chapter 3, for it is in benefit analysis that the route to differentiation is found. There is not much point in offering benefits that are expensive for you to provide but that are not highly regarded by customers. Consider using a matrix like the one in Figure 5-5 to classify your benefits. You will succeed by providing as many benefits as possible that fall into the top right-hand box.

Figure 5-5
Classification of Benefits

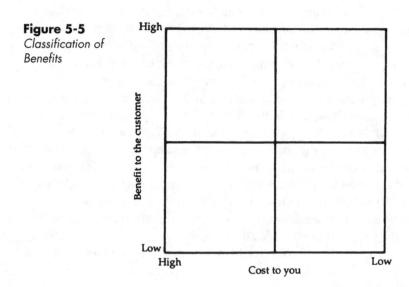

When setting marketing objectives, it is essential for you to have a sound grasp of your position and your competitors' positions in your markets and to adopt appropriate postures for the several elements of your business, all of which may be different. It may be necessary, for example, to accept that part of your portfolio is in the "disaster" box (box 4). You may well be forced to have some products there, for example, to complete your product range to enable you to offer your more profitable products. If this is true you must adopt an appropriate stance toward these products and set your marketing objectives accordingly, using, when appropriate, the guidelines given in Figure 5-3.

Finally, here are some general guidelines to help you think about competitive strategies:

1. Know the terrain on which you are fighting (the market).
2. Know the resources and capabilities of your enemies (competitive analysis).
3. Do with determination something that the enemy is not expecting.

What gap needs to be filled? ## WHERE TO START (GAP ANALYSIS)

Figure 5-6 illustrates what is commonly known as *gap analysis*. If the corporate sales and financial objectives are greater than the current long-range forecasts, a gap exists that has to be filled.

The *operations gap* can be filled in two ways:

1. Improved productivity—for example, reduce costs, improve the sales mix, increase prices, reduce discounts, and improve the productivity of the sales force
2. Market penetration—for example, increase usage and increase market share

The *new strategies gap* can be filled in three ways:

1. Market extension—for example, find new user groups, enter new segments, expand geographic area
2. Product development
3. Diversification—for example, selling new products to new markets

A fourth option, of course, is to reduce the objectives.

Gap analysis is best conducted in two separate steps. Step 1 is done for sales revenue only, so in the operations gap in Figure 5-6, reducing costs

Figure 5-6
Gap Analysis

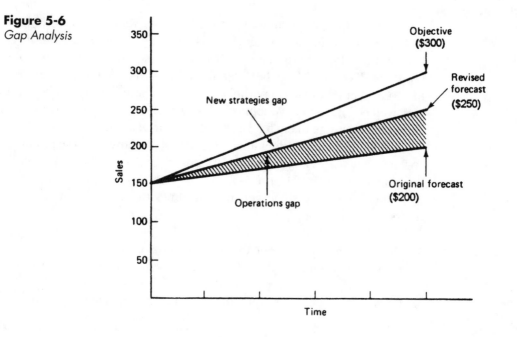

is not relevant. Step 2 has the same stages as step 1, but in this step the profit and cost implications of achieving the sales growth are examined. A detailed, step-by-step method for completing both steps is given in chapter 12.

If improved productivity is one method by which the profit gap is to be filled, care must be taken not to take measures such as reducing marketing costs by a constant, say, 20 percent overall. The portfolio analysis undertaken during the marketing audit stage almost always indicates that this amount would be totally inappropriate in some product and market areas, for which increased marketing expenditure may be needed, whereas for others 20 percent reduction in marketing costs may not be sufficient.

As for sales growth options, market penetration should always be a company's first option. It makes sense to attempt to increase profits and cash flow from existing products and markets initially, because this is usually the least expensive and the least risky method. For its present products and markets, a company has developed knowledge and skills that it can use competitively.

It makes sense in many instances to move along the horizontal axis for further growth before attempting to find new markets. The reason is that it normally takes many years for a company to get to know its customers and markets and to build a reputation. Reputation and trust, embodied in the company's name or in its brands, are rarely transferable to new markets, in which other companies are already entrenched.

The marketing audit should ensure that the method chosen to fill the gap is consistent with the company's capabilities and should build on its strengths. Selling a product to existing channels by the existing sales force is far less risky than introducing a new product that requires new channels and new selling skills. New products should be consistent with the company's known strengths and capabilities. Gillette's acquisition of Duracell is an example of good fit. Gillette's line of personal care products moves through the same channels as batteries.

Diversification is the riskiest strategy of all.

Caution in diversification also applies to a company's production, distribution, and people. New products should be as consistent as possible with the company's known strengths and capabilities. The use of existing plant capacity is generally preferable to use of new processes. The amount of additional investment also is important. Technical personnel are highly trained and specialized, and whether their competence can be transferred to a new field must be considered. A product that requires new raw materials may also require new handling and storage techniques, which may prove expensive.

Going into new markets with new products (diversification) is the riskiest strategy of all because new resources and new management skills have to be developed. The history of business is replete with examples of companies that failed when they moved into areas in which they had little or no experience.

The Ansoff matrix is not a simple four-box matrix because there are degrees of technological newness as well as degrees of market newness. Figure 5-7 illustrates the point. It also underlines why any movement should generally aim to keep a company as close as possible to its present position, rather than moving it to a totally unrelated position, except in the most unusual circumstances. Nevertheless, the product life cycle phenomenon inevitably forces companies to move along one or more of the axes of the Ansoff matrix if they are to continue to increase their sales and profits. A key question to be asked is how this important decision is to be made, given the risks involved.

One final point to make about gap analysis based on the Ansoff matrix is that when completed, the details of exactly how to achieve the objectives still have to be worked out. This is the purpose of the strategic marketing plan. Gap analysis represents a useful starting point in mapping out the general route, which is why we suggest you start here, rather than going to the trouble of preparing a strategic marketing plan only to have to change it later.

Figure 5-7
Ansoff Matrix: Degrees of Newness

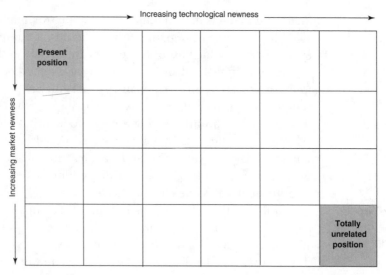

NEW PRODUCT DEVELOPMENT, MARKET EXTENSION, AND DIVERSIFICATION

Sooner or later all organizations need to move along one or both axes of the Ansoff matrix. The objective is to maximize synergy, the $2 + 2 = 5$ effect. The starting point is the marketing audit, leading to the SWOT (strengths, weaknesses, opportunities, and threats) analysis. Development of any kind will be firmly based on the company's basic strengths and weaknesses. External factors are the opportunities and threats facing the company. Once this important analytical stage is successfully completed, the more technical process of opportunity identification, screening, business analysis, and, finally, activities such as product development, testing, and entry planning can take place, depending on which option is selected. The important point is that no matter how thoroughly subsequent activities are carried out, unless the objectives of product development and market extension are based firmly on an analysis of the company's capabilities, they are unlikely to be successful in the long term. Figure 5-8 illustrates the process.

The criteria selected will be generally consistent with the criteria used for positioning products or businesses in the nine-cell portfolio matrix described in chapter 4. The list shown in Table 4-1 (which is also consistent with the marketing audit checklist) can be used to select the criteria that are most important. A rating and weighting system can then be applied to opportunities identified to assess their suitability or lack thereof. The crite-

Figure 5-8
*The Marketing
Planning Process*
See Figure 5-9
for the key to ab-
breviations.

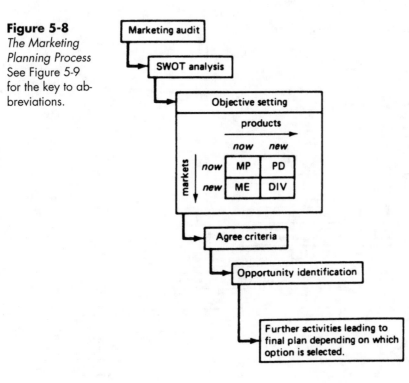

ria selected and the weighting system used should be consistent with the
SWOT analysis.

Figure 5-9 depicts the relation between the new product development process and the marketing audit and SWOT analysis. New product
development can be seen as a process consisting of the following seven
steps:

1. **Idea generation** The search for product ideas to meet company objectives
2. **Screening** A quick analysis of the ideas to establish which ideas are
   relevant
3. **Concept testing** Checking with the market to see whether the new
   product ideas are acceptable
4. **Business analysis** Detailed examination of the idea in terms of its
   commercial fit in the business
5. **Product development** Making the idea into hardware
6. **Testing** Market tests necessary to verify early business assessments
7. **Commercialization** Full-scale product launch, committing the
   company's reputation and resources

Figure 5-9 *The New Product Development Process*

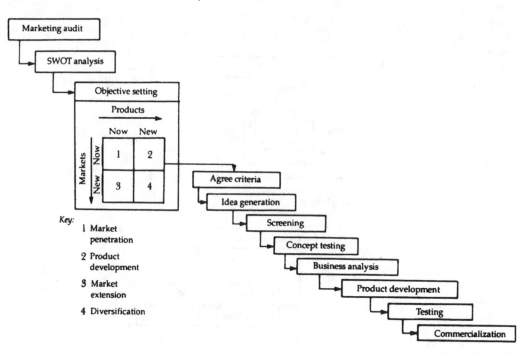

Key:

1 Market penetration

2 Product development

3 Market extension

4 Diversification

MARKETING STRATEGIES

What is marketing strategy? Essentially, it is a set of integrated actions in pursuit of value for customers and competitive advantage for the firm. We agree with Michael Porter that strategy is a unique and valuable position involving different and integrated activities.[1] Strategy requires decisions about which customers to target, what kind of products to offer, at what price, and where. A strategy involves significant trade-offs: decisions about what not to do. For example, Southwest Airlines, unlike its full-service competitors, does not provide first- and business-class service or meal or baggage-transfer service. The company's unique position is its ability to provide low-cost (passed on to customers as low-priced) on-time service on short-haul domestic routes in the U.S. Southwest's strategy has not been successfully copied by any challenger: the company's set of integrated activities is a major barrier to competitors who cannot easily duplicate the Southwest value system.

What a company wants to accomplish in terms of factors such as market share and volume is a marketing objective. How the company intends

1. Porter, Michael E. "What is Strategy?" *Harvard Business Review,* November–December 1996, pp. 60–78.

to achieve its objectives is strategy. Strategy is the overall route to the achievement of specific objectives and should describe the means by which objectives are to be reached, timing, and the allocation of resources. Strategy does not spell out the detailed plans and tactics that will be required.

There is a clear distinction between strategy and detailed implementation, or tactics. Strategy is the route to achievement of specific objectives and describes how objectives are to be reached. Marketing strategy reflects the company's best opinion of how it can most profitably apply its skills and resources to the marketplace. Strategy is inevitably broad in scope. The plan that stems from a strategy spells out action and timing and contains the detailed contribution expected from each department.

There is a similarity between strategy in business and strategic military development. One looks at the enemy, the terrain, and the resources under command and decides whether to attack the whole front, to attack an area of enemy weakness, to feint in one direction while attacking in another, or to encircle the enemy's position. The policy and mix, the general direction in which to go, and the criteria for judging success all come under the heading of strategy. The action steps are tactics.

In marketing the same commitment, mix, and types of resources, guidelines, and criteria that must be met all come under the heading of strategy. For example, the decision to use distributors in all but the three largest market areas, in which company salespeople will be used, is a strategic decision. The selection of particular distributors is a tactical decision.

Marketing strategies are the means by which marketing objectives are achieved and are generally concerned with the four major elements of the marketing mix. These are as follows:

- **Product** The general policies for product branding, positioning, deletions, modifications, additions, design, packaging

General Content of Strategy Statements

1. Policies and procedures relating to the products to be offered, such as number, quality, design, branding, packaging, and labeling
2. Pricing levels to be adopted, margins, and discount policies
3. Advertising and sales promotion, the creative approach, the type of media, types of displays, the amount to spend
4. The emphasis to be placed on personal selling, the sales approach, sales training
5. The distributive channels to be used and the relative importance of each
6. Warehousing, transportation, inventories, service levels in relation to distribution

- **Price** The general pricing policies to be followed for product groups in market segments
- **Place** The general policies for channels and customer service levels
- **Promotion** The general policies for communicating with customers under the relevant headings, such as advertising, sales force, sales promotion, public relations, exhibitions, direct mail

The following list of marketing strategies (in summary form) covers most of the options open under the headings of the four Ps:

Product
- Expand the line
- Change performance, quality, or features
- Consolidate the line
- Standardize design
- Positioning
- Change the mix
- Branding

Price
- Change price, terms, or conditions
- Skimming policies
- Penetration policies

Promotion
- Change advertising or promotion
- Change selling

Place
- Change delivery or distribution
- Change service
- Change channels
- Change the degree of forward integration

Chapters 6 through 9 are devoted to a much more detailed consideration of promotion, pricing, and distribution. Those chapters describe what should appear in advertising, sales, pricing, and place plans. This detail is intended for those whose principal concern is the preparation of a detailed one-year operational or tactical plan. The relation between chapters 6 through 9 and the strategic plan is in the provision of information to enable the planner to delineate broad strategies under the headings outlined earlier. This book contains no chapter on product management because all product options are covered in earlier chapters, particularly chapter 4 in the discussion of product audit. Estimating in broad terms the cost of strategies and delineating alternative plans are covered in more detail in chapter 10.

Marketing strategies: most critical, difficult parts of the entire marketing process

Formulating marketing strategies is one of the most critical and difficult parts of the entire marketing process. It sets the limit of success. Communicated to all management levels, marketing strategies indicate strengths to be developed and weaknesses to be remedied and in what manner. Marketing strategies enable operating decisions to bring the company into alignment with the emerging pattern of market opportunities that previous analysis has shown will offer the highest prospect of success.

This chapter confirms the need for setting clear, definitive objectives for all aspects of marketing and shows that marketing objectives themselves have to derive logically from corporate objectives. This practice allows all concerned with marketing activities to concentrate their particular contribution on achieving the overall marketing objectives to facilitate meaningful and constructive evaluation of all marketing activity.

Once agreement has been reached on the broad marketing objectives and strategies, those responsible for programs can proceed to the detailed planning stage and develop the appropriate overall strategy statements into sub-objectives. For the practical purpose of marketing planning, overall marketing objectives have to be broken down into sub-objectives. Meeting the sub-objectives will enable the company to meet overall objectives. Breaking down the overall objectives makes the problem of strategy development manageable.

Plans constitute the vehicle for getting to the destination along the chosen route, or the detailed execution of the strategy. The term *plan* often is synonymous in marketing literature with the terms *program* and *schedule*. A plan that contains detailed lists of tasks to be completed, together with responsibilities, timing, and cost, is a detailing of the actions to be taken and of the expected financial results of taking them.

QUESTIONS SUCCESSFUL COMPANIES ASK

1. What is the principal purpose of our company's existence?
2. Has there been any product and market extension during the past ten years that has not been a good fit with our integrated activities? Why?
3. How would we conduct a gap analysis? A competitor analysis? A SWOT analysis?
4. Who should be involved in formulating our marketing strategy? How open should we be in sharing our strategic marketing plans with all levels of the organization?

6

The Communication Plan: Advertising and Sales Promotion

Chapter 6 explains the difference between personal and impersonal communication and provides a method for deciding on the communication mix. It shows how to prepare an advertising plan and discusses in some detail what advertising objectives are and how to set them. There is a brief discussion of the role of the diffusion of innovation curve in advertising. The sales promotion plan is then introduced. There is a section on how the plan can be used, the different types of plans, and the strategic role of the plan. Finally, there is a section on how to prepare a sales promotion plan.

DIFFERENT FORMS OF COMMUNICATION

Now that we have explored the important area of marketing objectives and strategies, let us turn our attention to the question of how we communicate with customers, both current and potential.

We communicate in two basic ways.
Organizations communicate with their customers in a wide variety of ways. The two main categories of communication are as follows:

Impersonal communication, such as advertising, point-of-sale displays, promotions, and public relations

Personal (or direct person-to-person) communication, such as the face-to-face meeting between a salesperson and a customer

Companies have at their disposal a variety of communication techniques, which may be used either singly or in a combination (the *communication mix*) as the situation demands, to achieve maximum effect within budget constraints.

Companies that communicate successfully with customers continually experiment with the mix of communication techniques they use in an attempt to become more cost effective in this important, sometimes expensive, part of their business. This chapter discusses advertising and sales promotion with the objective of deciding how to prepare detailed plans for these important elements of the marketing mix.

DECIDING ON THE COMMUNICATION MIX

Advertising is paid for impersonal communication using media such as newspapers, magazines, television, radio, the Internet, and billboard posters. A number of problems have to be considered before any decision can be made about whether to spend money on advertising at all, let alone how to spend it. The first question that has to be grappled with is how to determine the communication mix. To help with this question, consider two separate surveys on how industry buys. These are shown in Tables 6-1 and 6-2.

Note the following:

1. More than one person has an influence on what is bought.
2. Salespeople do not manage to see all the important influencers.
3. Companies obtain the information with which they make their decisions from a variety of sources, only one of which is the salesperson.

The buying process is complicated by the number of people involved and the amount of time taken.

The industrial buying process is complicated by the fact that it is not just one person who is involved. Industrial buying is a decision-making process that can involve a large number of people and that can take considerable time. It is possible to split the decision-making process into several distinct steps, as follows:

1. The buyer organization recognizes it has a problem and works out a general solution. For example, the design team of a new plant or piece of machinery may decide that they need a specialist component that cannot be provided by the company's existing suppliers.

TABLE 6-1 Buying Influence According to Company Size

Number of Employees	Average Number of Influences	Average Number of Contacts Made by Salespeople
0–200	3.42	1.72
201–400	4.85	1.75
401–1000	5.81	1.90
1000+	6.50	1.65

Source: McGraw-Hill

TABLE 6-2 Sources of Information

	% Small Companies	Large Companies
Trade and technical press	28	60
Salesperson—calls	47	19
Exhibitions	8	12
Direct mail	19	9

Source: Maclean Hunter

2. The characteristics and quantity of what is needed are worked out. This outline design process specifies performance and particular characteristics such as weight, size, and operating conditions.
3. A specification is drawn up.
4. A search is conducted for possible sources of supply. This may merely involve a search of suppliers' catalogs to buy a component from inventory, or a complete new product may have to be designed.
5. Potential suppliers submit plans and products for evaluation.
6. After the necessary trials, suppliers are selected.
7. An order is placed and the product eventually delivered.
8. The goods supplied are checked against specification.

Not all these phases are used in every buying decision. When something is being bought for a new project, all the phases are used.

In cases of simple reorders of a product that has been bought before, the search and even bidding processes may not be necessary. The newness of the decision to the buying organization also determines which types of people and how many are involved at each stage. *Newness* is a function of the following factors:

- The complexity of the product
- The commercial uncertainty surrounding the outcome of the purchase

The more newness there is in both these dimensions, the more people are involved and the higher their status. If product complexity is high but commercial uncertainty is low, the more important role is that of the design engineer and technologist. If newness is low in both dimensions, purchasing officers tend to dominate the process.

When faced with a new buy situation, a salesperson is involved with a large number of people over a long period, helping, advising and informing, always trying to influence the decision process and to build a growing commitment toward his or her product. An example of this pro-

Purchasing a Telecommunication System

1. The president proposes to replace the company's telecommunication system.
2. Corporate purchasing and corporate telecommunication departments analyze the company's needs and recommend likely matches with potential selling organizations.
3. Corporate telecommunication department and data processing managers have an important say about with which system and firm the company deals. Other company executives also have a key influence on this decision.
4. All employees who use the telecommunication equipment are consulted.
5. The chief information officer selects, with influence from others, the supplying company and the system.

cess at work can be seen in the above example of the purchase of a telecommunication system.

It is important to identify the people with a high degree of influence on the purchase decision and the specific benefits each influencer wants. It is not possible to determine the precise role of advertising versus, for example, personal selling until a company understands how its potential customers buy and who are the important people to contact at the different stages in the buying process. Financial and administrative people are involved at a different stage from the engineers, and they need different kinds of information. For example, price, performance characteristics, delivery, before and after sale service, reputation and reliability, guarantees, and payment terms are not relevant to all people at all stages in the buying process.

The first point, then, is that a firm must understand the buying process of the markets to which it addresses itself. There are many models for helping with this process, but essentially you use a simple model that enables you to answer the following questions:

1. Who are the people with a high degree of influence on the purchase decision?
2. What specific benefits does each important influencer want?

Figure 6-1 provides a logical approach to analyzing an organization. This approach can be used equally effectively in either a product or a service company. When you have performed the analysis for your customers and potential customers, it should be comparatively easy to do the following:

Figure 6-1 *Customer Analysis Form (Adapted from P. Robinson, C. W. Farris, and G. Wind,* Industrial Buying and Creative Marketing, *Allyn & Bacon, 1967)*

Customer analysis form

Customer _____

Salesperson _____

Address _____

Products _____

Telephone number _____

Buy class: New buy   Straight re-buy   Modified re-buy

Date of analysis _____

Date of reviews _____

Member of decision-making-unit (DMU) Buy phase / Name	Production	Sales and marketing	Research and development	Finance and accounts	Purchasing	Data processing	Other
1. Recognizes need or problem and works out general solution							
2. Works out characteristics and quantity of what is needed							
3. Prepares detailed specification							
4. Searches for and locates potential sources of supply							
5. Analyzes and evaluates bids, plans, products							
6. Selects supplier							
7. Places order							
8. Checks and tests product							

Factors for consideration
1. Price
2. Performance
3. Availability
4. Back-up service
5. Reliability of supplier
6. Other users' experience
7. Guarantees and warranties
8. Payment terms, credit, or discount
9. Other, e.g., past purchases, prestige, image

1. Group the customers in some way (segmentation)
2. Determine the most cost-effective way of communicating benefits to each group

Only after the analysis is conducted can qualitative judgments be made about the relative cost-effectiveness of, for example, advertising versus personal selling, which, incidentally, are not mutually exclusive in anything but unusual circumstances. Table 6-3 lists communication objectives that contribute to a total marketing program, the objective of which is to achieve profitable sales.

We can now turn our attention specifically to advertising.

TABLE 6-3 Communication Objectives

Objective	To
Education and information	Create awareness Inform Get inquiries
Branding and image building	Get company name in file Create company image Reach personnel
Affecting attitudes	Ease the selling task Get press coverage Overcome prejudice Influence end-users
Loyalty and reminding	Reduce selling costs Achieve sales

PREPARING THE ADVERTISING PLAN

For many years, people believed that advertising worked in a simple way—the advertiser sent a message and the target received it and understood it. Research, however, has shown that in an overcommunicated society, the process is more complex. Advertising is not the straightforward activity that many people believe it to be.

Perhaps the greatest misconception of all about advertising is that objectives for advertising for the purpose of measuring effectiveness should be set in terms of sales increases. Naturally, we hope that advertising will have an important influence on sales levels, but in most circumstances advertising is only one of a host of important determinants of sales levels, such as product quality, prices, customer service levels, and the competence of the sales force. In general, it is inappropriate to set sales increases as a direct objective for advertising. What objectives can be set for advertising? Start by agreeing that one needs to set objectives for advertising for the following reasons:

To set the budget for advertising

To determine the target audience

To determine the content of advertisements

To decide what media to use

To decide on the frequency of advertising

To decide how to measure the effectiveness of advertising

These decisions can be summarized as follows:

- Why (objectives)
- Who (target)
- What (copy platform)
- Where (media)
- How (creative platform)
- When (timing)
- How much (budget)
- Schedule
- Response
- Evaluation

ADVERTISING OBJECTIVES

Research has shown that many companies set objectives for advertising that advertising cannot achieve on its own. For example, it is unreasonable to set as an objective "to convince our target market that our product is best" if it is clear to the world that someone else's product is better. You cannot blame your advertising agency if this objective is not achieved.

The first step is to decide on reasonable objectives for advertising. The question to ask is: Is it possible to achieve the objective through advertising alone? If the answer is yes, it is an objective for advertising. If the answer is no, it is not an objective for advertising.

Setting reasonable, achievable objectives is the first and most important step in the advertising plan. All the other steps in the process of put-

What Can Advertising Through Media Do?

- Convey information
- Alter perceptions, attitudes, image, position
- Create desires
- Establish connections (e.g., powdered cream and coffee)
- Direct actions
- Provide reassurance
- Remind
- Give reasons for buying
- Demonstrate
- Generate inquiries

ting together the advertising plan flow naturally from this process. You can summarize the steps by asking the following questions:

Who

- is the target audience?
- What does the audience already know, feel, believe about us and our product or service?
- What does the audience know, feel, believe about the competition?
- What sorts of people compose the audience? How do we describe and identify them?

What

- response do we want to evoke from the target audience?
- are the specific communication objectives?
- do we want to say, make the audience feel, believe, understand, know about buying or using our product or service?
- are we offering?
- do we not want to convey?
- are the priorities of our objectives?
- Are the objectives written down and agreed by the company and advertising agency?

How

- are our objectives to be embodied in an appealing form?
- What is our creative strategy or platform?
- What evidence do we have that this is acceptable and appropriate to our audience?

Where

- is the most cost-effective place to expose our communication (in cost terms related to our audience)?
- is the most beneficial place for our communication (in expected response terms related to the quality of the channels available)?

When

- are our communications to be displayed or conveyed to our audience?
- What is the reasoning for our scheduling of advertisements and communications over time?
- What constraints limit our freedom of choice?
- Do we have to fit in with other promotional activity for our products or services supplied by our company? Other products or serv-

ices supplied by our company? Competitors' products? Seasonal trends? Special events in the market?

Result

- What results do we expect?
- How would we measure results?
- Do we intend to measure results and if so, do we need to do anything beforehand?
- If we cannot say how we are going to measure precise results, could our objectives not be sufficiently specific or not communication objectives?
- How are we going to judge the relative success of our communication activities (good, bad, indifferent)?
- Should we have action standards?

Budget

- How much money do the intended activities require?
- How much money is going to be made available?
- How are we going to control expenditure?

Schedule

- Who is to do what and when?
- What is being spent on what? Where and when is it being spent?

The role of advertising usually changes during the life cycle of a product. For example, the process of persuasion itself cannot usually start until there is some level of awareness about a product or service in the marketplace. Creating awareness is, therefore, usually one of the most important objectives early in a life cycle. If awareness has been created, interest in learning more usually follows.

Attitude development now begins in earnest. This might involve reinforcing an existing attitude or changing previously held attitudes to create interest in the product. This role tends to become more important later in the product life cycle, when competitive products are trying to establish their own niches in the market. The aim is to get the prospect to consider trying the product and then becoming a repeat purchaser of the product.

DIFFUSION OF INNOVATIONS

Research into the progress of any product along the diffusion curve can be useful, particularly for advertising and personal selling (see Figure 4.3). You can aim your early advertising and sales effort specifically at innovators. Once the first 3 percent of innovators have adopted your product, there is a good chance that the early adopters will try it, and once the 8 to 10 percent point is reached, the champagne can be opened, because there is a good chance that the rest will adopt your product.

What are a customer's specific characteristics?

The general characteristics of opinion leaders are that they are venturesome, socially integrated, cosmopolitan, socially mobile, and privileged. Ask yourself, What are the specific characteristics of these customers in our particular industry? You can tailor your advertising message specifically for them.

Advertising is not directed only at consumers. It can be directed at channels, shareholders, news media, employees, suppliers, and government, all of whom have an important influence on the success of a firm.

SALES PROMOTION

The term *advertising* can be defined as all paid-for, nonpersonal communication in measured media. This includes television, radio, print, outdoor media, online media, and cinema. *Sales promotion* is a specific activity, defined as the making of a featured offer to defined customers within a specific time limit.

Different Kinds of Sales Promotions

The many and varied types of sales promotions are listed in Table 6-4. Each of these different types is appropriate for different circumstances and each has advantages and disadvantages. For example, with a promotion that consists of a bonus of a free case of product, it is possible to measure precisely both the cost of the extra cases and the additional volume resulting from the offer. This promotion is fast and flexible, is effective when the customer is profit conscious, can be made to last as long as needed, and is simple to set up, administer, and sell. This promotion also has no cumulative value to the customer, is unimaginative, and can often be seen as a prelude to a permanent price reduction.

Great care is necessary in selecting a scheme appropriate to the objective.

The Strategic Role of Sales Promotion

Sales promotion is an important part of marketing strategy, but it is one of the most mismanaged of all marketing functions. Because sales promotion is essentially used as a tactical device, it often amounts to little more

TABLE 6-4 Types of Sales Promotions

Target market	Type of promotion					
	Money		Goods		Services	
	Direct	Indirect	Direct	Indirect	Direct	Indirect
Consumer	Price reduction	Coupons Vouchers Money equivalent Competitions	Free goods Premium offers (e.g., 13 for 12) Gifts Trade-in offers	Stamps Coupons Vouchers Money equivalent Competitions	Guarantees Group participation events Special exhibitions and displays	Cooperative advertising Stamps Coupons Vouchers for services Events admission Competitions
Trade	Loyalty schemes Incentives Full-range buying	Extended credit Delayed invoicing Sale or return Coupons Vouchers Money equivalent	Gifts Trial offers Trade-in offers	Coupons Vouchers Money equivalent Competitions	Guarantees Group participation events Free services Risk reduction schemes Training Special exhibitions Displays Demonstrations Reciprocal trading schemes	Stamps, coupons Vouchers for services Competitions
Sales force	Bonus Commission	Coupons Vouchers Points systems Money equivalent Competitions	Gifts	Coupons Vouchers Points systems Money equivalent	Free services Group participation events	Coupons Vouchers Points systems for services Event admission Competitions

than a series of spasmodic gimmicks that lack coherence. The same management that organizes sales promotion usually believes that advertising should conform to an overall strategy. Perhaps this is because advertising has always been based on a philosophy of building long-term brand franchise in a consistent manner, whereas the basic rationale of sales promotion is to help the company retain a tactical initiative. Even so, there is no reason why there should not be a strategy for sales promotion, so that each promotion increases the effectiveness of the next. In this way a bond between seller and buyer is built up, so that the tactical objectives are linked in with some overall plan and so that there is generally a better application of resources.

There is widespread acknowledgment that sales promotion is one of the most mismanaged of all marketing functions. The objectives for each promotion should be clearly stated. Such objectives may include trial, repeat purchase, distribution, display, or a shift in buying peak to combat competition. The following process should apply:

- Select the appropriate technique
- Pretest
- Mount the promotion
- Evaluate in depth

Spending must be analyzed and categorized according to type of activity (e.g., special packaging, special point-of-sale material, loss of revenue through price reductions).

Checklist for Promotional Instruction

Heading	Content
Introduction	Briefly summarize content—What? Where? When?
Objectives	Marketing and promotional objectives for new product launch
Background	Market data, justification for technique, other relevant matters
Promotional offer	Detail the offer (e.g., special pricing structure, premium). Be brief, precise, and unambiguous.
Eligibility	Who? Where?
Timing	When is the offer available? Call, delivery, or invoice dates?
Date plan	Assign dates and responsibilities for all aspects of plan before start date
Support	Special advertising, point of sale, presenters, brochures, public relations, samples
Administration	Invoicing activity, free sample invoice lines, warehouse stocks, premium ordering and reordering procedure, cash drawing procedures
Sales plan	Targets, incentives, effect on routing, briefing meetings, telephone sales
Sales presentation	Points to be covered in call
Sales reporting	Procedure for collection of required data not otherwise available
Assessment	Method of evaluation of promotion

As for the sales promotional plan itself, the objectives, strategy, and brief details of timing and costs should be included. It is important that too much detail not appear in the sales promotional plan. Detailed promotional instructions follow as the marketing plan unfurls. For example, the checklist on page 112 outlines the kind of detail that eventually is circulated. However, only an outline appears in the marketing plan.

Additional Needs

The following tasks are usually designed to be performed by salespeople as an aid to selling the promotion:

- Summary of presentation points
- Price structures and profit margins
- Summary of offer
- Schedules of qualifying orders
- Blank order forms for suggested orders
- Copies of brochures

Also required by the sales force may be:

- Samples of new or existing product
- Demonstration specimen of premium item
- Special report forms
- Returns of cash or premiums issued

It is assumed that the sales manager has agreed to the broad principles of the promotion.

To achieve its marketing objectives, a company must communicate with existing and potential customers. It can do this directly, face to face, generally using a sales force, or indirectly, using advertising, promotion, and point of sale displays. The choice of communication mix is based on what is going to be most cost-effective in terms of achieving objectives, that is, whatever achieves the best results per given cost.

QUESTIONS SUCCESSFUL COMPANIES ASK

1. In creating our advertising plan, we might ask the following:
   - Who is our target market? What do we know about this market?
   - What are our objectives?

- What is our creative platform?
- Where is the best place to put our communication? Will it be cost-effective? Does it generate the right image?
- When will our communication be displayed? Is this the best time?
- Does it fit with our other activities?
- What do we expect to achieve? How will we measure this?

2. Who should create the advertising? Who should create the media plan?
3. How will we measure the effectiveness of our advertising?

7 The Communication Plan: Sales

Chapter 7 discusses the importance and role of personal selling in the marketing mix and goes on to outline a method for determining the number of salespeople required. Quantitative and qualitative sales force objectives are defined, and a method for improving sales force productivity is provided. Sales force management is discussed briefly. Finally, the reader is shown how to prepare the sales plan.

Personal selling has an important strategic role to play in communication between a company and its customers. To have a chance for success, management must be able to answer the following kinds of questions:

- How important is personal selling?
- What is the role of personal selling in the marketing mix?
- How many salespeople do we need?
- What do we want the sales force to do?
- How should the sales force be managed?

These and other questions are considered in this chapter as important determinants of the sales plan.

HOW IMPORTANT IS PERSONAL SELLING?

Most organizations had an organized sales force long before they introduced formal marketing activity of the kind described in this book. In spite of this fact, sales force management has traditionally been a neglected area of marketing management. There are several possible reasons. One is that not all marketing and product managers have had experience in a personal selling or sales management role; consequently, these managers often underestimate the importance of efficient personal selling.

Another reason for neglect of sales force management is that sales personnel themselves sometimes encourage an unhelpful distinction between sales and marketing by depicting themselves as "the infantry." After all, is there not something slightly daring about dealing with real live customers as opposed to sitting in an office surrounded by marketing sur-

115

veys, charts, and plans? Such reasoning is misleading. Unless a good deal of careful marketing planning has taken place before the salesperson makes his or her effort to persuade the customer to place an order, the probability of a successful sale is much reduced.

The suggested distinction between marketing "theory" and sales "practice" is further invalidated when one considers that profitable sales depend not only on individual customers and individual products but also on groups of customers (that is, market segments) and on the supportive relation between products (that is, a carefully planned product portfolio). Another factor to be taken into account in this context is the constant need for the organization to think in terms of where future sales will come from, rather than to concentrate solely on present products, customers, and problems.

Personal selling is a crucial part of the marketing process. In our experience, many companies lack planning and professionalism in their sales forces. Salespeople frequently have little idea of on which products and on which groups of customers to concentrate, have little knowledge about competitive activity, do not plan presentations well, rarely talk to customers in terms of *benefits*, make too little effort to close the sale, and make many calls without clear objectives. Even worse, marketing management is rarely aware that this important and expensive element of the marketing mix is not being managed effectively.

The fact that many organizations have separate departments and executives for the marketing and sales activities increases the likelihood of such failures of communication. Surveys show that more money is spent by many companies on their sales forces than on advertising and sales promotion combined. Personal selling, then, is a vital and expensive element in the marketing mix.

The solution to the problem of poor sales force management can be found only in the recognition that personal selling is a crucial part of the marketing process. It must be planned and considered as carefully as any other element. It is an excellent idea for any manager responsible for marketing to go out into a territory at least one week each year and attempt to persuade customers to place orders. It is a good way to find out what customers really think of the organization's marketing policies.

THE ROLE OF PERSONAL SELLING

Personal selling is part of the *communication mix.* (Other elements of the communication mix include advertising, sales promotion, public relations, direct mail, and exhibitions.) The surveys described in chapter 6 show that organizations cannot leave the communication task only to the sales force. As with advertising, the same question remains, How does the organization define the role of personal selling in its communication mix? The answer lies in a clear understanding of the buying process that operates in the company's markets.

Match information required to information given.

The efficiency of any element of communication depends on achieving a match between information required and information given. To achieve this match, the marketer must be aware of the different requirements of different people at different stages of the buying process. This approach highlights the importance of ensuring that the company's communications reach *all* key points in the buying chain. No company can afford to assume that the actual sale is the only important event.

To determine the precise role of personal selling in the communication mix, the company must identify the main influencers in each purchase decision and find out what information the influencers are likely to need at different stages of the buying process.

Most institutional buying decisions consist of many separate phases, from the recognition of a problem through performance evaluation and feedback on the product or service purchased. The importance of each of these phases varies according to whether the buying situation is a first-time purchase or a routine repurchase. The information differs in each case (see chapter 6).

Once an order has been obtained from a customer and there is a high probability of a rebuy, the salesperson's task changes from persuasion to *reinforcement.* All communication at this stage should contribute to underlining the wisdom of the purchase. The salesperson may also take the opportunity to encourage consideration of other products or services in the company's range.

In different markets, different weight is given to the various forms of communication available. In the grocery business, for example, advertising and sales promotion are extremely important elements in the com-

---

Advantages of Personal Selling

1. Personal selling is a two-way form of communication. It gives the prospective purchaser the opportunity to ask questions of the salespeople about the product or service.

2. The sales message itself can be flexible and therefore can be tailored to the needs of individual customers.

3. The salesperson can use in-depth product knowledge to relate his or her message to the perceived needs of the buyer and to deal with objections as they arise.

4. Most important, the salesperson can ask for an order and, perhaps, negotiate price, delivery, or special requirements.

munication process. However, the food manufacturer must maintain an active sales force, which keeps in close contact with the retail buyers. This retail contact ensures vigorous promotional activity in the chain. In the wholesale hardware business, frequent and regular face-to-face contact with retail outlets through a sales force is a key determinant of success. In industries in which there are few customers (such as capital goods and specialized process materials) an in-depth understanding of the customer's production process has to be developed. Personal contact is of paramount importance. In contrast, many fast-moving industrial goods are sold into fragmented markets for diverse uses. In this area, forms of communication other than personal selling take on added importance.

DETERMINING THE REQUIRED NUMBER OF SALESPEOPLE

The organization begins its consideration of how many salespeople it needs by finding out exactly how work is allocated at present. Start by listing all the things the current sales force actually does. These might include opening new accounts, servicing existing accounts, demonstrating new products, taking repeat orders, and collecting debts. This listing is followed by an investigation of alternative ways of carrying out these responsibilities. For example, telephone direct marketing is an alternative to sales calls, particularly for repeat business. The sales force can thus be freed for missionary work. This can be an attractive alternative to using the sales force. IBM, for example, is shifting more of its selling to direct marketing because the cost of keeping a "blue suit" in the field exceeds $200,00 per year. This means that the cost of a typical sales call is more than $200.00.

Can debts be collected by mail or by telephone? Can products be demonstrated at exhibitions or showrooms? It is only by asking these kinds of questions that we can be certain we have not fallen into the common trap of committing the company to a decision and then seeking data and reasons to justify the decision. At this stage, the manager concentrates on collecting relevant, quantified data and then uses judgment and experience to help in making a decision.

All sales force activities can be categorized according to three basic headings. A salesperson does the following:

- Makes calls
- Travels
- Performs administrative functions

These tasks constitute what can be called the *workload*. If you decide what constitutes a reasonable workload for a salesperson, in hours per month, then you can begin to measure how long current activities take and the exact extent of the current workload. This measurement can be performed by an independent third party or, preferably, by the salespeople themselves. All they have to do for one simple method of measurement is to record distance traveled, time in and out of calls, and the outlet type. The data can then be analyzed to indicate the average duration of a call by outlet type, the average distance traveled in a month, and the average speed according to the nature of the territory (that is, city, suburbs, or country). With the aid of a map, the company can assign existing customers on a trial-and-error basis together with the concomitant time values for clerical activities and travel. In this way, equitable workloads can be calculated for the sales force, building in, if necessary, spare time for investigation of potential new sales outlets. There are, of course, other ways of measuring workloads. One large consumer goods company used its work study department to measure the effectiveness of the sales force. The results of this study are summarized in Table 7-1.

TABLE 7-1 Breakdown of a Salesperson's Total Daily Activity

		Percent of Day		Minutes per Day	
Outside call time	Drive to and from route	15.9		81	
	Drive on route	16.1		83	
	Walk	4.6		24	
	Rest and breaks	6.3		32	
	Pre-call administration	1.4		7	
	Post-call administration	5.3		27	
			49.6		254
Inside call time	Business talks	11.5		60	
	Sell	5.9		30	
	Conversation	3.4		17	
	Receipts	1.2		6	
	Miscellaneous	1.1		6	
	Drink	1.7		8	
	Waiting	7.1		36	
			31.9		163
Evening work	Office work	9.8		50	
	Recording sales	3.9		20	
	Plan route	4.8		25	
			18.5		95
			100.0		8 hr 32 min.

Table 7-1 shows the company how a salesperson's time was spent and approximately how much of the time was actually available for selling. One immediate action taken by the company was to initiate a training program that enabled more time to be spent on selling as a result of better planning. Another was to improve the quality of the sales performance while face-to-face with customers. Armed with this kind of quantitative data, a company finds it easier to determine how many salespeople are needed and how territories can be equitably allocated.

DETERMINING THE ROLE OF SALESPEOPLE: QUANTITATIVE OBJECTIVES

Whatever the method used to organize a salesperson's day, there is always comparatively little time available for selling. In these circumstances, it is vital that a company know as precisely as possible what it wants its sales force to do. Sales force objectives can be either *quantitative* or *qualitative*.

Objectives: quantitative or qualitative

The principal quantitative objectives are concerned with the following measurements:

- How much to sell (the value of unit sales volume)
- What to sell (the mix of product lines to sell)
- Where to sell (the markets and individual customers that will take the company toward its marketing objectives)
- Desired profit contribution (when relevant and when the company is organized to compute this)
- Selling costs (in compensation, expenses, supervision, for example)

The first three types of objectives are derived directly from the marketing objectives (see chapter 6), which constitute the principal components of the sales plan.

There are, of course, many other kinds of quantitative objectives that can be set for the sales force, including the following:

- Number of point-of-sale displays organized
- Number of letters written to prospects
- Number of telephone calls to prospects
- Number of reports turned in or not turned in
- Number of trade meetings held
- Use of sales aids in presentations
- Number of service calls made

- Number of customer complaints
- Safety record
- Collections made
- Number of training meetings conducted
- Competitive activity reports
- General market condition reports

Salespeople may also be required to fulfill a coordinating role between a team of specialists and the client organization. A company selling mining machinery, for example, employs a number of general salespeople who establish contacts and identify which ones are likely to lead to sales. Before entering into negotiations with any client organization, the company selling the machinery may feel that it needs to call in a team of highly specialized engineers and financial experts for consultation and advice. The salesperson in this company needs to identify where specialist help is required and coordinate the people who become involved in the negotiation. Most objectives are subservient to the main objectives, which are associated directly with what is sold and to whom.

QUALITATIVE OBJECTIVES

Qualitative objectives can be a potential source of problems if sales managers try to assess the performance of the sales force along dimensions that include abstract terms such as "loyalty," "enthusiasm," "cooperation," and so on, since such terms are difficult to measure objectively. In seeking qualitative measurements of performance, managers often resort to highly subjective interpretations, which cause resentment and frustration among those being assessed.

However, managers can set and measure qualitative objectives that actually relate to the performance of the sales force on the job. It is possible, for example, to assess the skill with which salespeople apply their product knowledge on the job, or the skill with which they plan their work, or the skill with which they overcome objections during a sale interview. While still qualitative in nature, these measures relate to standards of performance understood and accepted by the sales force.

Given such standards, it is not too difficult for a competent field sales manager to identify deficiencies, to get agreement on them, to coach in skills and techniques, to build attitudes of professionalism, to show how to self-train, to determine which training requirements cannot be tackled in the field, and to evaluate improvements in performance and the effect of any past training.

One consumer goods company with thirty field sales managers discovered that most of them were spending much of the day in their offices engaged in administrative work, most of it self-made. The company proceeded to take the offices away and insisted that the sales managers spend most of their time in the field training their salespeople. To assist them in this task, they trained them how to appraise and improve salespeople's performance in the field. There was a dramatic increase in sales and consequently in the sales managers' own earnings. This rapidly overcame their resentment at losing their offices.

IMPROVING THE PRODUCTIVITY OF THE SALES FORCE

Many salespeople might secretly confess to a proclivity to call more frequently on large customers who give them a friendly reception and less frequently on those who put barriers in their way. If you classify customers according to friendliness and size, you can develop a simple matrix to help you decide where to direct your effort. In Figure 7-1 the boxes that offer the greatest potential for increased sales productivity are boxes 4 and 5; boxes 1 and 2 receive a maintenance call rate. Boxes 7 and 8 receive an alternative strategy to establish whether hostility can be overcome. If the alternative approaches fail, a lower call rate may be appropriate. Box 9 is the "do not bother" box. Boxes 3 and 6 receive the minimum attention consistent with your goals. None of this is meant to indicate definitive

Figure 7-1

Improving Sales Force Productivity

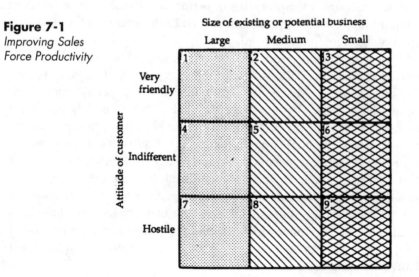

rules about call frequencies, which always are a matter of management judgment. The sole purpose of the grid is to prompt questions about assumptions about call frequencies for existing and potential accounts to check that you are not using valuable time that could be more productively used in other directions.

PREPARING A SALES PLAN

No two sales plans contain precisely the same headings. However, there are some general guidelines. Table 7-2 is an example of setting objectives for an individual salesperson. These objectives are the logical result of breaking down the marketing objectives into actual sales targets.

All companies set overall objectives, which leads to the development of specific marketing objectives. This chapter discusses personal selling in the context of overall marketing activity. This approach leads to the following hierarchy of objectives: *corporate objectives, marketing objectives, sales objectives* (Figure 7-2).

The benefits to sales force management of following this approach can be summarized as follows:

1. Coordination of corporate and marketing objectives with actual sales effort
2. Establishment of a circular relation between corporate objectives and customer wants
3. Improvement of sales effectiveness through an understanding of the corporate and marketing implications of sales decisions

To summarize, the sales force is a vital but very expensive element of the marketing mix and as much care should be devoted to its management as to any other area of marketing. This is most likely to be achieved

A Sales Force Cannot Be Managed in Isolation

The sales force of a company manufacturing stainless steel containers was selling almost any kind of container to almost anybody who could buy. This caused severe production planning and distribution problems throughout the business, down to the purchase of raw materials. Eventually the company's profitability was seriously affected. The sales force was finally instructed to concentrate on certain kinds of products and on certain kinds of user industries. This decision led to economies of scale throughout the whole organization.

TABLE 7-2 Objectives for the Individual Salesperson

Task	The Standard	How to Set the Standard	How to Measure Performance	What to Look For
1. To achieve a personal sales target	–Sales target per period of time for individual groups or products	–Analysis of • territory potential • individual customers' potential –Discussion and agreement between salesperson and manager	–Comparison of individual salesperson's product sales against targets	–Significant shortfall between target and achievement over a meaningful period
2. To sell the required range and quantity to individual customers	–Achievement of specified range and quantity of sales to a particular customer or group of customers within an agreed time period	–Analysis of individual customer records of • potential and • present sales –Discussion and agreement between manager and salesperson	–Scrutiny of • individual customer records • observation of selling in the field	–Failure to achieve agreed objectives –Complacency with range of sales made to individual customers
3. To plan travel and call frequencies to achieve minimum practicable selling cost	–To achieve appropriate call frequency on individual customers –Number of live customer calls during a given time period	–Analysis of individual customers' potential –Analysis of order/call ratios –Discussion and agreement between manager and salesperson	–Scrutiny of individual customer records –Analysis of order/call ratio –Examination of call reports	–High ratio of calls to an individual customer relative to that customer's yield –Shortfall on agreed total number of calls made over an agreed time period
4. To acquire new customers	–Number of prospect calls during time period –Selling new products to existing customers	–Identify total number of potential and actual customers who could produce results –Identify opportunity areas for prospecting	–Examination of • call reports • records of new accounts opened • ratio of existing to potential customers	–Shortfall in number of prospect calls from agreed standard –Low ratio of existing to potential customers
5. To make a sales approach of the required quality	–To exercise the necessary skills and techniques required to achieve the identified objective of each element of the sales approach –Continuous use of sales material	–Standard to be agreed in discussion between manager and salesperson related to company standards –Regular observations of field selling using a systematic analysis of performance in each stage of the sales approach	Regular observations of field selling using a systematic analysis of performance in each stage of the sales approach	–Failure to • identify objective of each stage of sales approach • develop specific areas of skill, correct weakness • use of support material

(Based on the original work of Stephen P. Morse while at Urwick Orr and Partners)

Figure 7-2
Objectives for the Individual Sales-person

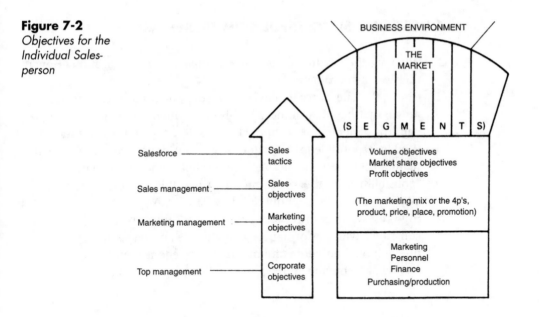

if intuitive sense, which is associated with experience, can be combined with the kind of logical framework of thinking outlined herein (Figure 7-3). Personal selling provides the face-to-face element of the communication mix. There are things it can achieve that advertising and promotion cannot. For example, salespeople can be flexible in front of the customer and ask for an order. However, personal selling has to be seen in the context of the total communication mix.

Figure 7-3
Effective Sales Management: Thinking + Data + Intuition

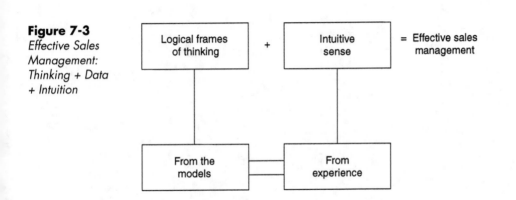

QUESTIONS SUCCESSFUL COMPANIES ASK

1. What are the key functions of salespeople in our organization? How is their work coordinated?
2. How is the sales force deployed—by geographical territory, by product range, by type of customer? Is this deployment optimal? What other patterns of deployment should be considered by our organization?
3. Who is responsible for the sales force in our organization? What is the relation between this post of responsibility and other marketing responsibilities in the organization? Does this cause any problems? When problems arise, how can they be solved?
4. How can we maximize sales performance? Incentives can be rewards consistent with performance, giving praise and recognition when it is due, minimal boredom and monotony, freedom from fear or worry, a feeling of belonging, and a sense of doing a useful job.

8 The Pricing Plan

Chapter 8 begins by cautioning against cost-plus pricing approaches. It discusses the pricing decision in the context of portfolio management, product life cycle analysis, and product positioning. Costs are explored as an input for pricing policy, as is pricing for channels. There is a section on pricing for competitive advantage through value-in-use pricing. The reader is shown how to prepare a pricing plan.

Pricing has two boundaries: the upper boundary of competition and lower boundary of cost.

Pricing is a critical element of the marketing plan, the first thing to say about pricing is that there are two boundaries that must always be kept in mind: the upper boundary of competition and the lower boundary of cost. In general the price offer cannot be greater than a comparable offer from the competition nor can it be, in the long term, less than cost. That having been said, it remains to be established what is a comparable offer from the competition and what are costs. Neither is easy or simple to determine.

The pricing decision is important because price affects not only the margin through its impact on revenue but also the quantity sold through its influence on demand. In short, price has an interactive effect on the other elements of the marketing mix. It is essential that price be part of a conscious marketing plan with objectives that have been clearly defined. Although in some areas of the economy pricing may be determined by forces that are largely outside the control of corporate decision makers, prices in the marketplace are normally the result of decisions made by company managements. What should the decision be when accounting wants to increase the price of a product to increase margins while marketing wants to hold or even reduce the net selling price to increase market share? The answer appears to be simple. Get the calculator out and see which proposal results in the largest profit.

Pricing decisions affect the margins and quantities sold.

OBJECTIVES AND THE PRODUCT PORTFOLIO

Unfortunately, many arguments within firms about pricing take place in the sort of vacuum created when no one has bothered to specify the *objectives* to which pricing is supposed to be contributing. It is important that a company have a well-defined hierarchy of objectives to which all its activities and actions, including pricing, can be related. For example, corporate objectives may dictate that the generation of short-term profits is a requirement. (This may be because of the position of a particular business unit in a matrix in relation to other units in the same corporation. For example, a group decision may have been made to invest heavily in one business unit's growth and to fund this growth from one of their cash cow units elsewhere in their portfolio.)

Corporate objectives have an important influence on *marketing* objectives. In the same way, a company's marketing objectives for a particular product may dictate short-term emphasis on profitability rather than market share, which influences pricing strategy. This is a function of the product's position in relation to other products in the portfolio. For example, it may be that a product is one of many question marks, and the company has chosen others rather than this particular one in which to invest. This would result in a wish to make the largest possible contribution to profits from the product, and the pricing strategy would be used to reach this goal. The establishment of marketing objectives for any particular product is the starting point in any consideration of pricing.

PRODUCT POSITIONING

Price is one of the clearest signals a customer has of the value of the offer that a company is making. There must be a relation between price and perceived value. For example, several years ago Smirnoff was a popular national vodka brand not clearly positioned as a premium vodka. To change the positioning of Smirnoff, the company increased the price $1.00 a bottle, $0.50 of which was invested in advertising. The remaining $0.50 was dropped to the bottom line. The pricing change combined with the new advertising campaign successfully repositioned Smirnoff into the luxury vodka category, and sales and profits increased. Product positioning, then, is another consideration in the pricing decision.

COMPETITION AND POTENTIAL COMPETITION

All products have competitors and potential competitors that must be carefully considered in the pricing decision. Some firms launch new products at high prices to recover their investment costs only to find that they have created a price umbrella to which competitors adapt. The competitors then launch similar products at much lower prices. The competitors' lower prices enable them to take market share and move down the experience curve quicker, giving them a cost advantage. A lower launch price, with possibly a quicker rate of diffusion and hence a greater rate of experience, may make it more difficult for a potential competitor to enter the market profitably.

COSTS

Another key factor for consideration is costs—not only your costs but also those of your competitors. The conventional profit-maximizing model of economists tends to indicate that a price should be set at the point at which marginal cost equals marginal revenue. That is, the additional cost of producing and marketing an additional unit is equivalent to the additional revenue earned from its sale. The theory is indisputable, but the practice is difficult, if not impossible, to apply. This is largely because the economists assume that price is the only determinant of demand, whereas in reality this is not always so.

Without an accurate costing system, there is no point of reference to put pricing into perspective.

In practice, the costs of manufacturing or providing a service provide the basis for most pricing decisions, that is, a cost-plus method. The trouble with most cost-oriented pricing approaches is that they make little attempt to reconcile what the customer is prepared to pay with what it costs the company to be in business and make a fair return on its investment of resources. A company uses a cost-oriented approach when it aims for a certain return on costs. That is, the company sets itself a target level of profits at a certain projected level of sales volume. This type of approach involves a simple form of break-even analysis (Figure 8-1).

Figure 8-1
Break-even Analysis

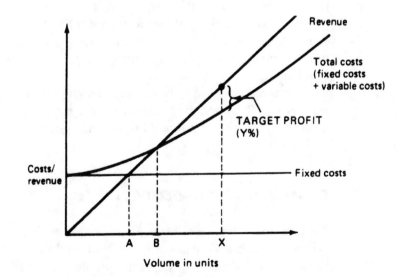

In Figure 8-1 fixed costs are shown as a straight line and all other costs are allocated on a cost-per-unit basis to produce an ascending curve. At point A, revenue covers only fixed costs. At point B, all costs are covered and any additional sales produce net profit. At point X, Y% target profit is being achieved. The problem with this approach to pricing is that it is assumed that at a given price a given number of products are sold, whereas in reality, the quantity sold depends on the price charged. Users of this model also assume a break-even *point,* whereas in most companies the best that can be said is that there is a break-even *area* at a given level of production. This approach, however, is useful for helping one to understand the relation between different kinds of costs.

By far the most common way of setting price is to use the cost-plus approach. One arrives at a price that yields margins commensurate with declared profit objectives. When making a pricing decision, consider a number of different costing options, for any one can be misleading on its own, particularly those that allocate fixed costs to all products in the portfolio. Often the basis of allocation is debatable, and an unthinking marketer may accept the costs as given and easily make the wrong pricing decision.

Remember, if you try to have the lowest price, someone will usually try to go even lower; this is a difficult battle to win.

Consider the following scenario. In difficult economic times, when cost savings are sought, unprofitable products are eliminated from the range. Unprofitable products are identified by the gross or net margins in the last complete fiscal year and by estimates of these margins against estimated future sales. However, because conventional cost accounting allocates the highest costs to high-volume products, these products show lower margins, so sometimes they are sacrificed. Product elimination, however, often saves only small amounts of direct costs, so the remaining products have to absorb higher costs, and the next profitability crisis appears. Product elimination also reduces the scale of operations and the product mix, so there is less incentive to invest, and the company is less competitive.

This is not intended to be an attack on any kind of total average costing method. Our intention is merely to advise caution and a broader perspective in the use of any kind of costing system as a basis for pricing decisions.

CHANNELS OF DISTRIBUTION

Channel intermediaries perform a number of functions. In return for their services, these intermediaries need to be rewarded; this reward is in effect the *margin* between the price of the product out of the factory and the

A number of devices are available for rewarding channel intermediaries. Most rewards take the form of discounts against a nominal price list. The types of discounts are as follows:

Trade discount A discount given against the price list for services made available by the intermediary, such as holding inventory, buying in bulk, and redistribution

Quantity discount A discount offered to intermediaries who order in large lots

Promotional discount The discount given to distributors to encourage them to share in the promotion of the products involved

Cash discount A cash discount of about 2.5 percent for payment within 10 days to encourage prompt payment of accounts

price the consumer pays. The total channel margin may have to be shared among several intermediaries and still have the product reach the consumer at a competitive price. Intermediaries live or die on the economics of their respective operations. The ideal reward structure in the marketing channel is to ensure that an acceptable rate of return on investment is earned at each level. This situation often is not achieved because of imbalances of bargaining power.

In a dynamic marketing channel, there is constant pressure on suppliers to improve margins. Because of these pressures, the use of margins should be seen as strategic as well as tactical. Margin management can be viewed as a series of trade-off decisions that determine how the total channel margin is split. The concept of the total channel margin is simple. The margin is the difference between the level of price at which you want to position your product in the ultimate marketplace and the cost of your product out of the factory. Who takes what proportion of this difference (Figure 8-2) is what margin management is about.

A company's channel requirements are met only if the company itself carries them out or if the company goes some way toward meeting

Figure 8-2
*Marketing
Objectives
and Channel
Margins*

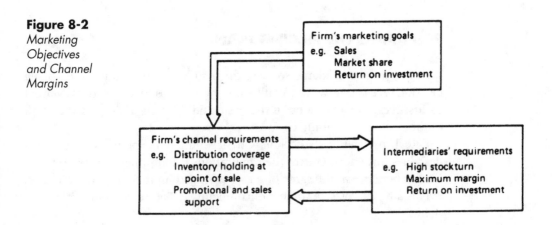

Figure 8-3
Pricing, Margin, and Profitability

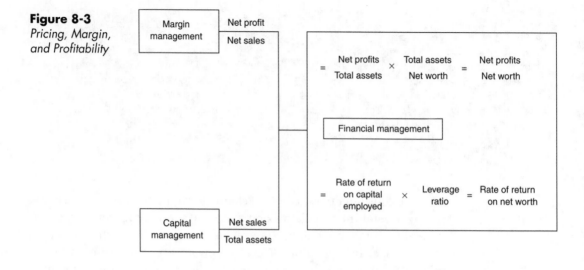

the requirements of an intermediary who can perform the functions on the company's behalf. The objective of a company is to trade margin to achieve its marketing goals. Such a trade-off need not lead to a loss of profitability. As Figure 8-3 shows, the margin is only one element in the determination of profitability, profitability being defined as the rate of return on net worth (net worth being stockholders' equity and capital reserves plus retained earnings).

By improving the utilization of capital assets (capital management) and by using greater leverage, it is possible to operate successfully on lower margins if this means that marketing goals can be achieved effectively.

PREPARING THE PRICING PLAN

We have so far considered some of the main issues relevant to the pricing decision. We can now try to pull all of these issues together. However, let us first recapitulate on one of the basic findings that underpins the work of the Boston Consulting Group.

Real costs generally decline with accumulated experience. Figure 8-4 describes this effect. One of the implications is that unless a firm accumulates experience at the same or a greater rate than the market as a whole, eventually its costs become noncompetitive. Figure 8-5 illustrates this point.

Figure 8-4
*Relation Be-
tween Costs
and Experience*

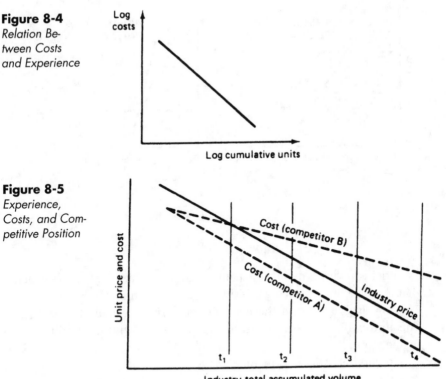

Figure 8-5
*Experience,
Costs, and Com-
petitive Position*

t = time period

**A skimming
policy intro-
duces a product
at a high initial
price and moves
down the expe-
rience curve at
a slower rate.
A penetration
policy intro-
duces a product
at a low initial
price and moves
down the expe-
rience curve at
a faster rate.**

A *skimming policy* involves setting a high initial price and moving down the experience curve at a slow rate. A *penetration policy* involves setting a low initial price, which, if successful, stimulates a high rate of product adoption and, therefore, a steep experience curve. Both policies are summarized in Figure 8-6.

The following circumstances favor a *skimming policy:*

- Demand is likely to be price inelastic.
- There are likely to be different price-market segments that appeal first to buyers who have a higher range of acceptable prices.
- Little is known about the costs of producing and marketing the product.

The following circumstances favor a *penetration policy:*

- Demand is likely to be price elastic.
- Competitors are likely to enter the market quickly.
- There are no distinct and separate price-market segments.
- There is the possibility of large savings in production and marketing costs if a large sales volume can be generated (the experience factor).

133

Figure 8-6
Skimming Policy and Penetration Policy

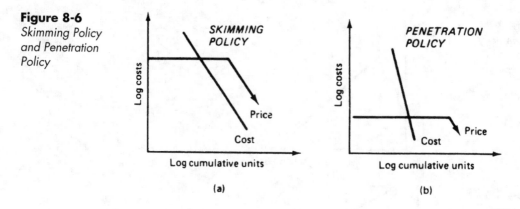

(a)

(b)

Pricing policy is determined after account has been taken of all factors that impinge on the pricing decision. These are summarized in Figure 8-7. The top diagram shows the discretionary pricing range for a company. The bottom diagram shows factors to take into account in reaching a pricing decision.

In general, pricing is included as part of product-segment plans. This can disguise some of the complex issues found in pricing.

QUESTIONS SUCCESSFUL COMPANIES ASK

1. When we last introduced a new product or service, how was the price established? Was the pricing decision correct? What additional information could we have used to help with the pricing decision? What would we do differently given the same circumstances?
2. How does our pricing strategy compare with that of our main competitors?
3. What is the true price of our product from the customer's perspective? Do we have a differential advantage (e.g., training costs, maintenance costs, energy consumption, disruption costs, consumable, floor space) over competing products, which offers greater value to customers in spite of our higher initial price?
4. What trends have occurred in margins in our industry? Are these trends acceptable? How will we remain price-competitive under expected future conditions?
5. Are we pricing our product/service optimally? Should we be adjusting our prices upward or downward?

Figure 8-7
Pricing Policy

Pricing alternatives for a hypothetical company

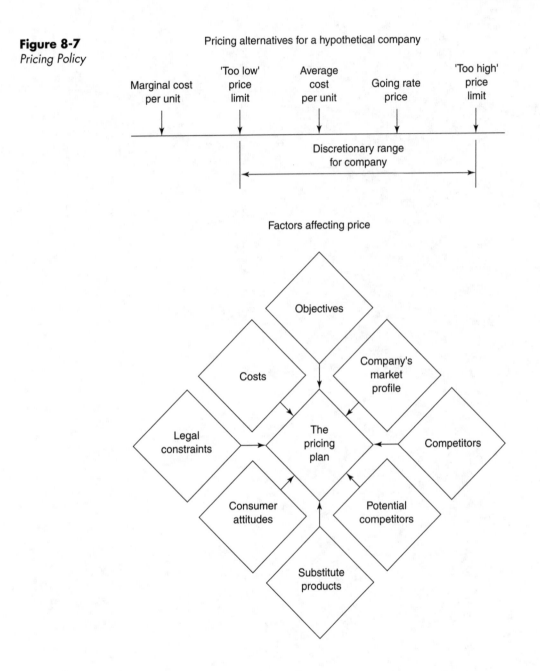

Factors affecting price

The Distribution Plan

Chapter 9 encourages readers to consider distribution in its widest sense as a critical aspect of marketing management rather than simple physical distribution management. The chapter goes on to explore the various components of the distribution mix. Marketing channels are discussed and a method for their evaluation is provided. The essential components of customer service are listed, and the reader is shown how to prepare a distribution plan.

Channels and physical distribution are well within the scope of marketing.

At Coca-Cola, one of the world's most admired and successful companies, channels are the cornerstone of the company's success. Coke's distribution around the world is a testament to the success of the company in creating a worldwide association of business partners who have put Coke within an arm's reach of desire around the world.

The topic of product distribution involves the following three decision areas, each of which is examined in turn:

1. How is the physical movement of our product organized?
2. Through what marketing channels do we reach our customers (or what channels do our customers use to acquire our products)?
3. What level of availability of our product does our customer require (and how well do we meet this requirement)?

PHYSICAL DISTRIBUTION

If a product is not available when and where the customer wants it, it will surely fail in the market.

The physical distribution function of a firm provides the place and time dimensions that constitute the third element of the marketing mix. This is depicted in Figure 9-1, which also shows its relation to the other utility-producing elements. The figures on the diagram are illustrative only, although they are realistic for some industries.

THE DISTRIBUTION MIX

In a typical manufacturing company with a formal distribution structure, the responsibility for distribution-related matters is spread across the

Figure 9-1
*Physical
Distribution*

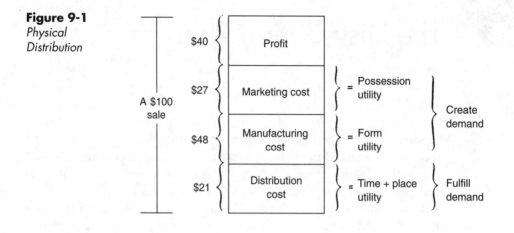

other functional departments. For example, production may control warehousing and transportation; marketing may control the channels through which the product moves, the levels of service provided to the customer, and inventory obsolescence; and the finance department may control communication, data processing, and inventory costs. Such a compartmentalized arrangement leads to each department's working to its own objectives, attempting to optimize its own particular activity oblivious of others or of the good of the company.

Introducing a formal distribution arrangement into the corporate organizational structure, although it does not completely eliminate interdepartmental friction, ensures that all distribution-related activities are organized under central control, allowing focus. A formal distribution arrangement is the basis of the total distribution concept, because it makes it possible to seek out potential trade-offs, that is, consciously to incur costs in one area to achieve benefit in another. For example, should a series of field warehouses be maintained, or would one suffice supplemented by an improved trucking operation? Of course, these types of potential trade-off situations place a heavy burden on the cost-reporting systems of a company.

A professional distribution manager has several variables to contend with in the search for trade-offs. These five areas constitute the *distribution mix* and the total cost of distribution within a company.

Each of these is examined briefly.

**Five areas make
up a company's
distribution
costs.**

Facilities

Decisions about facilities concern the problem of how many warehouses and plants should be established and where they should be located. For most companies it is necessary to take the location of existing plants and warehouses as given in the short term, but the question does arise in the long term or when new plants or warehouses are being considered. The principal marketing task is to forecast the nature, size, and geographic spread of demand. Increasing the number of field locations will result in an increase in trucking costs and a reduction in retail distribution costs. Another marketing task is to determine the customer service levels likely to be required to be able to make a decision about this particular trade-off.

Inventory

A large element of the total distribution costs of any company is the cost of inventory, which is often as high as 30 percent of its value per annum. This is because of items such as interest charges, deterioration, shrinkage, insurance, and administration. Decisions such as how much inventory to hold, where to hold it, and in what quantities to order are vital issues. Inventory levels also are instrumental in determining the level of service that the company offers the customer.

Transportation

The important aspects of the transportation decision concern issues such as the mode of transportation to be used, whether to own vehicles or lease them, how to schedule deliveries, and how often to deliver. Of the five distribution variables, transportation perhaps receives the greatest attention within the firm. It is certainly one of the more obvious facets of the distribution task.

Communication

Distribution involves not only the flow of materials through the distribution channel but also the flow of information. Communication involves areas such as the order-processing system, the invoicing system, and the demand-forecasting system. Without effective communication support, the distribution system will never be capable of providing satisfactory customer service at an acceptable cost.

Unitization

The way in which goods are packaged and then subsequently accumulated into larger unit sizes (e.g., a pallet load) can have considerable bearing on distribution economics. For example, the ability to stack goods on a pallet, which then becomes the unit load for movement and storage, can lead to considerable cost savings in terms of handling and warehousing. The use of containers as the basic unit of movement has revolutionized international transport and, to some extent, domestic transport. Mobile racking systems and front-end pricing by means of scanners are other unitization innovations that have had a dramatic effect on the way goods are marketed.

The right product at the right time.

MARKETING CHANNELS

The fundamental role of the distribution function of a company is to ensure that the right product is available at the right time. This implies organization of resources into channels through which the product moves to customers. A *marketing channel* is the route taken in the transfer of the title of a product or service from its original source of supply to its ultimate consumption. It is necessary to consider both the route of exchange and the physical movement route of the product—they may well be different.

Many companies use multiple marketing channels to reach their customers, often involving one or even several *intermediaries*. The role of an intermediary is to provide the means of achieving the widest possible market coverage at a lower unit cost. Many intermediaries hold stock and thereby share some of the financial risk with the principal (or supplier). Figure 9-2 shows that using an intermediary carries benefits for the manufacturer, but it also involves considerable costs, the most important of which is the loss of control that accompanies such a channel strategy.

Often considerable conflict exists between the objectives of suppliers and those of their distributors; this gives rise to conflict and suspicion in the relationship. Nevertheless, suppliers must evaluate the costs and benefits of each marketing channel potentially open to them and decide on a combination that best suits their type of business and the markets in which they are engaged. The alternatives depicted in Figure 9-3 have different cost-revenue profiles.

Any cost-benefit appraisal has to be undertaken in the widest context possible. It must consider questions of market strategy, the appropriate-

Figure 9-2
Marketing Channels and Use of an Intermediary

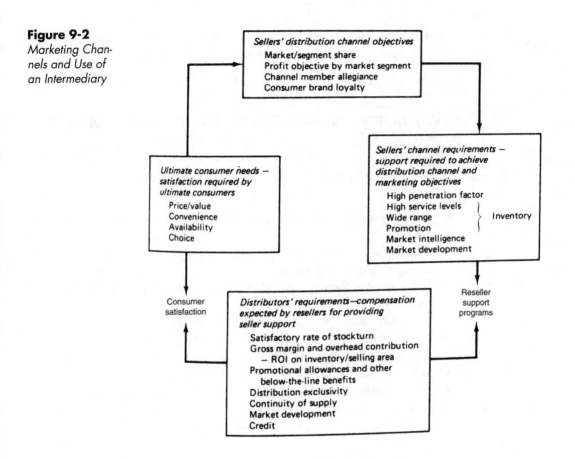

Figure 9-3
The Alternatives

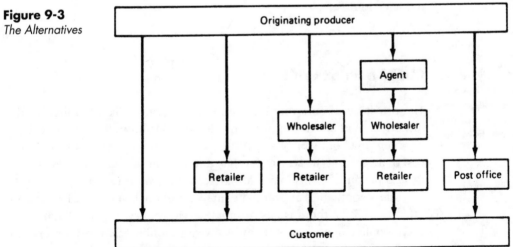

ness of the channel to the product, customer requirements, and the question of the comparative costs of selling and distribution.

EVALUATION CRITERIA FOR CHANNEL INTERMEDIARIES

Regardless of the type of intermediary to be used, there are a number of basic evaluation criteria. The following are examples:

- Does the intermediary now, or will it, sell to our target market segment?
- Is the sales force large enough and trained well enough to achieve our regional sales forecasts?
- Is the intermediary's regional location adequate in respect to the retail (and other) outlets serviced?
- Are promotional policies and budgets adequate?
- Does the intermediary satisfy customer after-sale requirements?
- Are the product policies consistent with our own?
- Does the intermediary carry competitors' lines?
- What are the inventory policies regarding width, depth, and cover?
- Is the intermediary credit worthy?
- Is distributor management receptive, aggressive, and flexible?

All the factors listed and others have to be considered in specific decisions about choice of intermediaries, which in turn is part of the overall channel selection issue.

Satisfying the customer encompasses every aspect of the relationship.

CUSTOMER SERVICE

The provision of customer service in all its forms is likely to involve the firm in large financial commitments. Figure 9-4 shows the typical relation between level of availability and the cost of providing it. As shown, the cost of increasing the service level by a small amount, say from 95 percent to 97.5 percent, results in a sharp increase in inventory costs.

Many companies appear to be unaware of the level of service they are offering, that is, there is *no* customer service policy as such. Even when such a policy does exist, the levels are quite often arbitrarily set and are not the result of careful market analysis.

Figure 9-4
Level of Availability and Cost

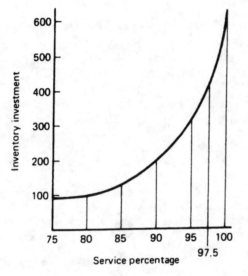

By carefully reviewing customer service policy, marketing can enhance its contribution to corporate profitability.

The question is: What level of availability should be offered? This question is relatively simple to answer in theory but difficult to quantify and achieve in practice, because different product groups in different market segments can demand different levels of customer service.

In theory, at least, it is possible to say that service levels can continue to be improved as long as the marketing advantage that results continues to outrun the additional costs incurred. It is possible to draw an S-shaped curve (Figure 9-5) that suggests that with very high levels of customer service, customers are unable to differentiate small changes in the service offered. When a company is operating in this region, it is quite possibly incurring more costs than are necessary for the level of sales being achieved.

Figure 9-5
S-shaped Customer Service Curve

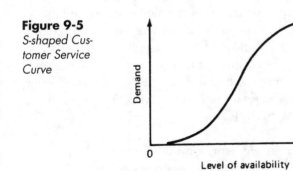

Questions to Determine Balance Between Costs and Benefits

1. How profitable is the product? What contribution to fixed costs and profits does this product make, and what is its sales turnover?
2. What is the nature of the product? Is it a critical item as far as the customer is concerned? That is, would stock-outs at the point of supply result in a loss of sales? Does the product have characteristics that result in high inventory costs?
3. What is the nature of the market? Does the company operate in a seller's or a buyer's market? How frequently is the product purchased? Are there ready substitutes? What are the inventory practices of the purchasers? Which markets and customers are growing and which are declining?
4. How profitable are the customers that constitute each segment?
5. What is the nature of the competition? How many companies are providing an alternative source of supply to our customers? What sort of service levels do they offer?
6. What is the nature of the channel of distribution through which the company sells? Does the company sell directly to the end-customer or through intermediaries? To what extent does the company control the channel and the activities of its members, such as stock levels and order policies?

For example, marketing and sales managers who insist on offering maximum service to all customers, no matter what the profitability and location of those customers, are doing their company a disservice. Somewhere between the costs and benefits involved in customer service, a balance has to be found. It is at that point that the additional revenue returns for each increment of service equal the extra cost involved in providing that increment. To attempt to ascertain this point of balance, certain information is required.

DEVELOPING A CUSTOMER SERVICE PACKAGE

Service encompasses every aspect of the relationship between manufacturers and their distributors or customers. Under this definition, price, sales representation, after-sale service, product range offering, and product availability are all dimensions of customer service—the total activity of servicing one's customer. It is fundamental for suppliers to derive their concept of customer service from a study of their customers' real needs.

Determining customer needs will almost certainly mean designing different customer service packages for different market groups. Six basic steps are involved in this process, as follows:

1. Define the important service elements (and subelements).
2. Determine customers' viewpoints on the service elements.

Components of Customer Service to Be Researched

- Frequency of delivery
- Time from order to delivery
- Reliability of delivery
- Emergency deliveries when required
- Stock availability and continuity of supply
- Complete filling of orders
- Advice on lack of availability
- Technical support
- Convenience of placing order
- Acknowledgment of order
- Accuracy of invoices
- Quality of sales representation
- Regular calls by sales representatives
- Manufacturer monitoring of retail inventory levels
- Credit terms offered
- Handling of customers' questions
- Quality of outer packaging
- Quality of inner package for in-store handling and display
- Consultation on new product or package development
- Regular review of product range
- Coordination among production, distribution, and marketing

3. Design a competitive package (and several variations, if necessary).
4. Develop a promotional campaign to sell the service package idea.
5. Pilot test a particular package and the promotional campaign being used.
6. Establish controls to monitor performance of the various service packages.

DEVELOPING THE DISTRIBUTION PLAN

Figure 9-6 shows the relation between the marketing and distribution plans. It makes organizational sense to make marketing responsible for distribution, because marketing is probably in the best position to make the difficult trade-off between very high levels of customer service and the high inventory-carrying costs associated with such levels.

WHAT IS INTEGRATED DISTRIBUTION MANAGEMENT?

Integrated distribution management is an approach to the distribution mission of a firm whereby two or more of the functions involved in moving goods from source to user are integrated and viewed as an interrelated system or subsystem for purposes of managerial planning, implementation, and control.

Figure 9-6
Relation Between Marketing and Distribution Plans

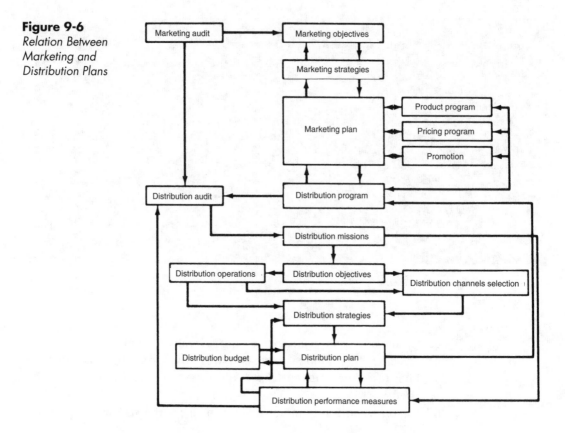

THE STARTING POINT

Like the more general marketing audit discussed in chapter 2, the distribution audit has two main parts—*internal* and *external*. Figure 9-7 illustrates the components of a distribution audit.

All of these decisions need not necessarily be located in one plan or be made by one person or department, but they have to be made and written somewhere in the company's plans.

Distribution objectives can be many and varied, but the following are considered basic for marketing purposes:
Outlet penetration by type of distribution

Inventory range and levels to be held
Distributor sales and sales promotion activities
Other specific customer development programs, such as incentives for distributors

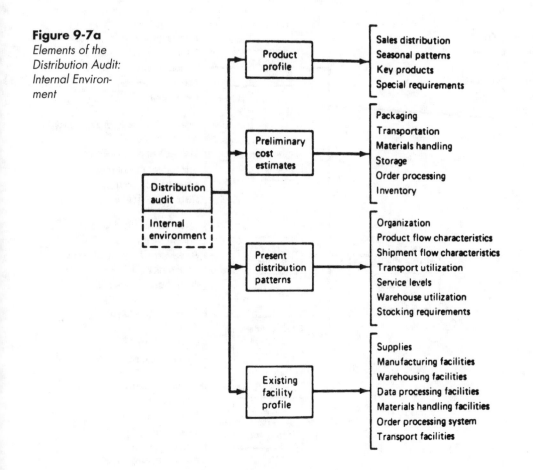

Figure 9-7a
Elements of the Distribution Audit: Internal Environment

Physical distribution ensures that products get to the right place, on time, and in the right condition. In some businesses, distribution costs can amount to 20 percent of the selling price. There are five components to

The following list illustrates a simple iterative approach to distribution planning that should help tighten what is often a neglected area of marketing management:

1. Determine marketing objectives.
2. Evaluate changing conditions in distribution at all levels.
3. Determine distribution tasks within overall marketing strategy.
4. Determine distribution policy in terms of type, number, and level of outlets to be used.
5. Set performance standards for the distribution organization.
6. Obtain performance information.
7. Compare actual with anticipated performance.
8. Adjust where necessary.

Figure 9-7b
*Elements of the
Distribution Audit:
External Environ-
ment*

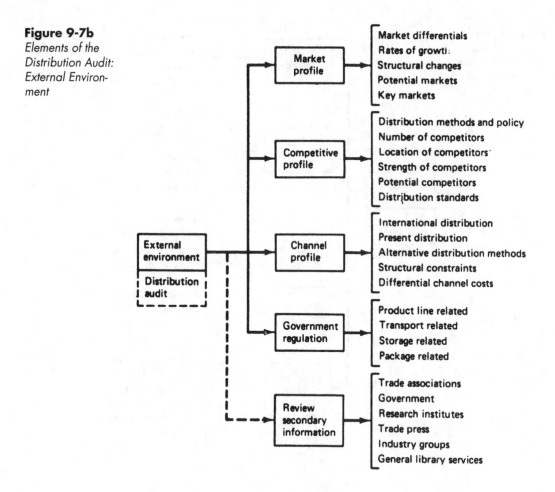

manage. From a range of possible distribution channels, choices should be
made for best competitive advantage.

QUESTIONS SUCCESSFUL COMPANIES ASK

1. What are the advantages and disadvantages of the channels currently
   used by our company?
2. Are there any cases in which the channels used may not be the most
   appropriate?
3. If we were new to the market, what channels would we use? What
   prevents us from making these changes?
4. Is logistics adequately represented at the senior management level in
   our organization? How can improvements be made?

5. What coordination takes place between physical distribution management and marketing management? How can problems be minimized?

6. How are decisions currently made concerning customer service levels? How does our customer service compare with that of competitors?

7. How might we make savings in our distribution system without reducing customer service?

10 Marketing Information, Forecasting, and Organizing for Marketing Planning

The first part of chapter 10 deals with the difference between market research and marketing research, how much to spend on it, the different forms of marketing research, database marketing, and marketing intelligence systems and how to organize them. Forecasting techniques are briefly covered. Finally, organizational structures for marketing planning are outlined and discussed and the cultural implications of marketing planning are discussed.

Chapter 11 discusses one of the most difficult aspects of marketing planning—actually making it all work by means of a system within the company. The actual *process* of marketing planning is simple in outline. Any marketing book tells us that planning consists of a situation review, assumptions, objectives, strategies, programs, measurement, and review. What some books *do not* tell us is that a number of contextual issues have to be considered that make marketing planning one of the most baffling of all marketing problems.

Until issues such as those listed in the box are understood, the other chapters in this book remain little more than interesting aspects of marketing planning. The purpose of chapter 10 is to help pick up all the pieces of the jigsaw puzzle and put them together to form a picture that can be seen and understood.

Major Marketing Issues

- *When* should marketing be done, *how often*, *by whom*, and *how*?
- Is marketing different in *large* and *small* companies?
- Is marketing different in *diversified* and *undiversified* companies?
- Is marketing different in *international* and *domestic* companies?

- What is the role of the *chief executive*?
- What is the role of the *planning department*?
- Should marketing planning be *top down* or *bottom up*?
- What is the relation between *operational* (one year) and *strategic* (long term) planning?

First, we need to set the scene and to fill in a few gaps concerning marketing information and the organizational side of marketing. Our research has shown that it is important to recognize at the outset the likely realistic constraints on the implementation of a marketing planning system. Two such constraints are marketing information and a company's organizational form, which are considered in this chapter. Chapter 11 demonstrates how marketing planning can be made to work by means of a system. It includes a discussion of the role of the chief executive and the planning department. Chapter 12 provides an actual marketing planning system that will enable you to operationalize the concepts, structures, and frameworks described in this book.

This chapter has the following two parts:

1. Marketing information and forecasting
2. Marketing organization

MARKETING INFORMATION AND FORECASTING FOR MARKETING PLANNING

Without information you will find it difficult to perform many of the fairly common-sense tasks discussed so far. A plan is only as good as the information on which it is based, which is why you need to make sure you know the right questions to ask, such as: Who are our customers? What is our market share?

Throughout this book, we emphasize that the profitable development of a company can only come from a continuous attempt to match the company's capabilities with customer needs. For the company to be sure that this matching process is taking place effectively, it is necessary that a flow of information be instituted between the customer and the firm. This is the role of marketing research.

The Difference Between Market Research and Marketing Research

Market research is concerned with specific research about markets. *Marketing research* is concerned with research into marketing processes. We are concerned here with marketing research, which has been defined by the American Marketing Association as the systematic gathering, recording, and analysis of data about problems related to the marketing of goods and services.

The words in the definition are important. The process has to be systematic, because it is necessary to have structured interaction between people, machines, and procedures designed to generate an orderly flow of pertinent information collected from sources both inside and outside the company, for use as the basis for decision-making in specified responsibility areas of marketing management.

Data by themselves (such as words, figures, pictures, and sounds) are of little use until they are combined with direction to become information. Without a purpose, a marketing problem to solve, information is not of much use either. One of the most important problems facing management today is a *surplus* of data and information, rather than too little. Which brings us to our definition of *intelligence,* which is information consumable and usable by management in converting uncertainty into risk.

Uncertainty occurs when any outcome is considered to be equally possible. When a probability can be assigned to certain outcomes, however, we are talking about *risk,* which is quantified uncertainty. A marketing manager might feel, for example, that a new product has a 90 percent likelihood of achieving 30 percent market share in its first year. The ability to make successful decisions is enhanced if one operates under conditions of risk rather than uncertainty.

Conversion of uncertainty into risk and the minimization of risk are among marketing management's most important tasks. In this process the role of marketing research is of paramount importance.

Intelligence = information consumable and usable by management in converting uncertainty into risk.

How Much to Spend on Marketing Research

Before looking at the different kinds of research available to the marketing manager, a book written about marketing planning should address the issue of the marketing research budget. Marketing information has to be produced, stored, and distributed, but it has a limited life—it is perishable. Like other resources, information has a value in use; the less the manager knows about a marketing problem and the greater the risk attached to a wrong decision, the more valuable the information becomes. This implies the need for a cost-benefit appraisal of all sources of marketing information. There is little point in investing more in such information than the return on the investment would justify.

Although costs are easy to identify, the benefits are difficult to pin down. Benefits can best be expressed in terms of the additional profits that might be achieved through identifying marketing opportunities and through the avoidance of marketing failures that can result without the use of information.

The decision about how much to spend on marketing information is not an easy one. On the one hand it would be foolhardy to proceed without any information at all. On the other hand, the cost of perfect information is prohibitive. One way of estimating how much to spend is based on the theory of probability and expected value. For example, if by launching a product you had to incur development costs of 1 million dollars and you believed there was a 10 percent chance that the product would fail, the maximum *loss expectation* would be 100,000 dollars (1 million dollars × 0.1). It is worth spending up to 100,000 dollars to acquire information that would help avoid such a loss. However, because perfect information is seldom available, it makes sense to budget a small sum for marketing research that effectively discounts the likely inaccuracy of the information. Such an approach can be a valuable means of quantifying the value of marketing research in a managerial context.

Forms of Marketing Research

Increasing sophistication in the use of the techniques available to the researcher, particularly in the handling and analysis of multivariate data, has made marketing research into a specialized function within the field of marketing management. Nevertheless, any company, irrespective of whether it has a marketing department, should be aware of tools that are available and where they may be used.

External and internal research: reactive and nonreactive

Marketing research can be classified as *external* or *internal*. External marketing information gathering is a complement to internal marketing analysis. External research activity is conducted within the competitive environment outside the firm. Much valuable intelligence also can be gained from internal marketing analysis in the form of sales trends, changes in the marketing mix such as price, and advertising levels. External marketing information gathering should always be seen as a complement to such internal information.

There is another basic split between *reactive* and *nonreactive* marketing research. Nonreactive methods are based on the interpretation of observed phenomena, or extant data. Reactive research involves proactive assessment in the marketplace.

The most widely used method of reactive marketing research involves asking questions by means of a *questionnaire* survey, which is a highly flexible instrument. The survey can be administered by an interviewer, by telephone, or by mail. All these different methods have advantages and disadvantages, and all have different cost consequences. For example, the greatest degree of control over the quality of the responses is obtained by having a researcher administer each questionnaire personally, but this is expensive and time consuming. Telephone interviews are quick and relatively inexpensive, but there is a severe limit to the amount of technical information that can be obtained by this means. The mail questionnaire is a much-favored method, but great care is necessary to avoid sample bias. For example, is there something special (and possibly therefore unrepresentative of the population) about those who reply to a mail questionnaire?

The most important potential pitfall with questionnaires lies in their design. Loaded questions and ambiguity are not always easily detectable. Even the order in which questions are asked can have a distortion effect on the answers. Such pitfalls can be reduced with *pilot testing.* Pilot testing involves administering the survey to a subgroup of the intended sample to isolate problems that may arise.

Sometimes it may be more appropriate to gather information not by large surveys but by small-scale, detailed studies that provide qualitative insights rather than quantitative conclusions. Focus groups can provide such insights. These are loosely structured discussions among a group that broadly represents the population in which the researcher is interested. A group leader attempts to draw from the group their feelings about the subject under discussion. In-depth one-on-one interviews can also can be conducted. This method is popular when information is required about specialized products or markets.

Experimentation is another type of reactive marketing research that can provide a valuable source of information about the likely market performance of new products or about the likely effects of variations in the marketing mix. Factors such as different product formulations and different levels of promotional effort can be tested in the marketplace to gauge different effects.

Market experimentation sometimes takes place in laboratory conditions, particularly in the case of advertising. Samples of the target audience are exposed to an advertisement, and their reactions are obtained. Eye cameras, polygraphs, and tachistoscopes are just some of the devices used to record physical reactions to marketing stimuli.

In contrast to such methods are those that are classified as *nonreactive* in that they do not rely on data derived directly from the respondent. Best known among nonreactive methods are retail audits and consumer panels, both widely used by consumer companies. *Retail audits* involve regular monitoring of a representative sample of stockists. At regular periods, researchers visit the stockists and record the current level of stock of the product group being audited and the delivery notes for any such goods delivered since the last visit. With the information on inventory levels from their last visit, it is now a simple matter to determine sales of the audited items with the following formula:

$$\text{Opening inventory} + \text{Deliveries between visits} - \text{Closing inventory} =$$
$$\text{Sales during the period}$$

A *consumer panel* is simply a sample group of consumers who record in a diary their purchases and consumption over a period of time. This technique has been used in industrial as well as consumer markets and can provide continuous data on use patterns and other useful data.

In many respects, the most important of all marketing research methods is the use of existing materials, particularly by means of *desk research,* which should always be the starting point of any marketing research program. A wealth of information can be obtained from published information such as government statistics, Organization for Economic Cooperation and Development, European Community, the United Nations, newspapers, technical journals, trade association publications, and published market surveys. Two or three days spent on desk research nearly always provides pleasant surprises for a company that believes it lacks information about its markets. When combined with internal sales information, this can be the most powerful research method open to a company.

Organizing Information to Develop Sound Plans

The practice of marketing planning is intrinsically difficult. The main concern is to choose markets to go after and to work out how to win them. The methods in this book can be applied to develop a plan that describes the marketing objectives and the winning strategies. The trouble is that such a plan can in theory be written without a scrap of supporting evidence. In practice, many plans are based on the flimsiest of evidence. The material in this section is heavily influenced by the work of Dr. Robert Shaw, of Shaw Consulting. Figures 10-1 through 10-3 and Table 10-1 are the copyright of Dr. Robert Shaw and are reproduced here with his kind permission.

Challenges: managing the complexity of the data and assessing the soundness of the evidence

Two challenges that involve evidence and information face executive management. The first challenge, faced by companies of any substantial size and diversity, is how to manage the complexity of the planning data. The question that arises is, How can the planners know very much about what is happening throughout the geographic regions with all the company's products and in all the market segments? Auditing the market requires that it be subdivided into many component parts according to

Figure 10-1
*One Hundred
Levels of Market
Subdivision and
Summarization*

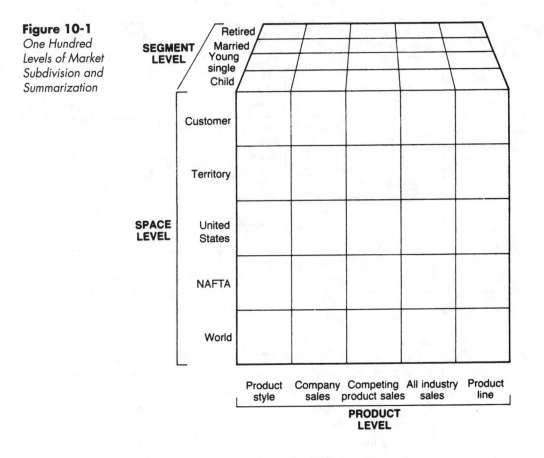

factors such as geography, product, and segment. Portfolio analysis necessitates reassembly of these components into a coherent structure.

The second challenge is how to assess whether a plan is based on good evidence or whether to ignore it as something "madding" which is neither based on accurate facts nor believed in consumption. In the process, planners need to match external facts about the market to internal facts and

Figure 10-2
*Planners Must
Match the Internal Categories
and Facts and
Figures to the
External Ones*

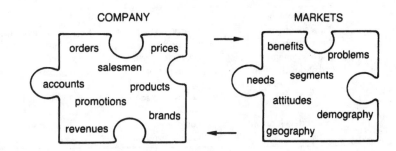

Figure 10-3
Information Flow in a Marketing System

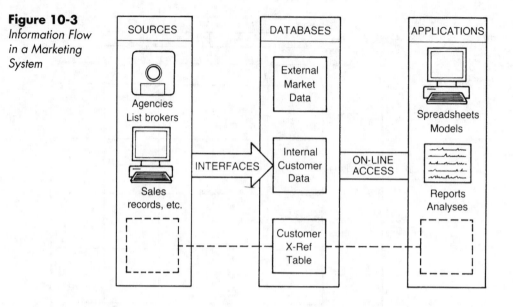

figures to create a clear and harmonious picture. It is rare, however, for the same categories to apply internally and externally, which makes the job of the planner especially difficult.

Some large companies have found a way to address both these problems thanks to the increased availability of information in computer databases and the power of computer software to make complexity manageable. Planners, however, must understand the limitations and weaknesses of the databases and master the software tools if they are to make the planning decisions sound as well as easy.

TABLE 10-1 Examples of Business Objectives and Segmentation Methods

Business Objective	Segmentation Method	Information Source
Market extension		
New locations	Geodemographics	Consumer research
New channels	Prospect profiles	Business research
New segments	Survey analysis	Market studies
Market development	Customer profiling	Sales ledger and added profile data
	Behavioral scoring	Models from internal data source
Product development	Factor analysis	Surveys
	Qualitative methods	Panels/discussion groups

Subdividing the Market: Data for Segmentation

As discussed in chapter 4, market segmentation is the process that subdivides the market into distinct groups of buyers who might merit separate products or marketing mixes. For each segment, a profile, and very often a meaningful and memorable name, is developed. Segmentation is effective only when it results in realistic commercial opportunities that can be targeted and measured in practice.

Market segments change over time as buyers' needs evolve and as new product offerings become available. The planner must constantly review new combinations of variables to see which reveal the best new opportunities. Segments are identified by means of application of successive variables to subdivide the market. As an illustration, a global telecom-

---

The following is a review of the steps involved in market segmentation:

1. *Segmentation objectives.* The researcher requires a clear, brief list of the business objectives. Different segmentation schemes may result from different objectives. If the objective is market extension, then the key segmentation variable may be income. If the objective is communication, then the key segmentation variable may be attitude.

2. *Desk research and market hypothesis.* The researcher collects readily available data and lays them out into a hypothetical map of the marketplace. This map contains many gaps and has been based on various assumptions. It suggests areas where more or better information has to be collected.

3. *Data collection and survey.* The researcher collects information from and about potential buyers. Examples are as follows:

- Buying or usage behavior
- Buyer attitudes to the product category
- Buyer characteristics, such as geographics, demographics, psychographics

This information can be obtained from the following sources:

- Public databases
- Proprietary databases (owned by research agencies)
- Questionnaires sent by mail
- Telephone research
- Face-to-face research

Internal customer data cannot be used in this context because they are not representative of the whole market, unless the company's customers are representative of all areas of the entire market. Large data samples often have to be collected to cover all combinations of variables. For example, in a survey in which the variables are sex, age (split into five categories), geography (ten regions), and products (five categories) with a minimum sample per combination of ten people, the survey would have to cover at least five thousand individuals to cover all combinations of segmentation variables.

4. *Data analysis.* A wide range of statistical techniques can be used to identify market segments. These include factor analysis, cluster analysis, and multiple regression. Techniques that go beyond the traditional limits of statistics include neural networks and pattern-finding algorithms.

5. *Profile definition.* Each segment is defined in terms of the key variables. Often the segments are named on the basis of a dominant characteristic.

munication company is interested in stimulating line usage among low users (segmentation variable: *product usage*). Low users are those who fear technology, those who are indifferent, and those who are positive toward technology (segmentation variable: *attitude*). Among those who feel positive are those with high incomes who can afford to use more service (segmentation variable: *income*). The telecommunication company may decide to aim at high income people who have a positive attitude but simply use the competitors' networks.

Who Should Be Responsible for the Segmentation Process?

Market research has traditionally played an important role in segmentation. However, it has often limited itself to "field and tab" methods, which are severely limited in their flexibility and do not support constant review of new combinations of segmentation variables. Field and tab methods involve the collection of data on *field* questionnaires, analysis of the data, and presentation of the results as *tabulations*. This approach is being superseded by in-house analysis supported by computer systems. There are three reasons for moving in-house—flexibility, competitive advantage, and technology.

Flexibility in Revision of Analysis

The market is changing too rapidly for the traditionally slow process of data collection, data analysis, and data presentation. Much data remain unanalyzed. Cost and time limit analysis to the simplest levels, often only cross tabulations. There is little opportunity to explore interesting features that emerge from this first stage. As target marketing moves closer to the ultimate market of one person, the facts produced by the old research are being replaced by models and information on demand.

More than one segmentation approach often is needed to fit the strategic objectives at all levels. This covers the advertising and sales promotion plan, the sales plan, the pricing plan, and the distribution plan. Cutting the data in many different ways to explore all the variables can be prohibitively expensive if done by an external research agency.

Along with inflexibility, lack of control in research is still a problem. Holding the data in house allows planners to reanalyze them time after time without the costs and delays associated with external agencies.

Competitive Advantage and Unique Segmentation Schemes

Standard segmentation schemes purchased from external agencies cannot provide substantial competitive advantage. Even if you gain advantage from these schemes today, your competitor can buy them tomorrow and rapidly catch up with you. A unique segmentation scheme is the best solution to a unique problem. Yet many agencies continue to offer standardized segmentation products to all their clients.

Take the automobile industry, for example. Henry Ford assumed that price was the dominant segmentation variable, then General Motors recognized different income and preference groups in the market. Much later, Japanese companies recognized the importance of car size and fuel economy. Recently manufacturers have identified vehicle type market as a segmentation tool, for example, the multipurpose vehicle market. The success of new entrants into the any market often results from the discovery of new segmentation possibilities in the market.

The Marketing Audit

Two challenges in conducting a marketing audit, as discussed in chapters 3 and 4, are as follows:

- Acquiring sound data from external and internal sources
- Matching external and internal categories

External Data Sources

One of the primary tasks in the external audit is to estimate market size and its breakdown by geography, product, and segment. This task is straightforward, given the vast quantities of market data that do exist. However, knowing where to begin to collect, store, and analyze data presents a real challenge. It helps to differentiate clearly between research on new markets and research on existing markets. Each presents a different set of problems in terms of data.

For *new markets*, data are comparatively scarce, and extrapolation from surveys is often the main source of information. Carefully designed analysis methods are necessary to resolve uncertainties introduced because samples are small. Models based on limited data and plausible assumptions have to be used to infer market size, structure, and dynamics.

161

For *existing markets,* public and agency-owned data sources can provide a rich and detailed picture. Behavioral data on buying patterns often are widely available; quite detailed information may be available on buyer attitudes and characteristics. Sophisticated statistical techniques that rely on large sample sizes can be used to infer market size, structure, and dynamics.

What Information Is Needed to Support a Marketing Strategy?

The answer to this question is something of a conundrum. The information needed depends on the marketing objectives that form the strategy. If you change the strategic marketing objectives, you may need different kinds of information to support your strategy. Table 10-1 illustrates how different objectives require different supporting information.

The Main Components of the Marketing System

External market data purchased from external agencies such as governmental agencies, market research firms, and list brokers

Internal customer data collected from sales records and other internal sources, such as customer service, field sales, and telesales. These data are coded and segmented in such a way that market share figures can be calculated by means of comparison with external data.

Customer reference table, which is needed to make the system work effectively. The table identifies customers (as defined by marketing) and provides a cross-reference to sales record accounts. Whenever a new sales account is established, the cross-reference table is used to determine the customer associated with the account. This avoids the need for costly manual matching after the account is established. The customer reference table also is used by marketing applications as a standard reference.

A *database* that holds all three of the foregoing data types. It is structured by means of *data modeling,* the process by which data are organized into the component types that marketing wants, not the structure that finance or anyone else provides. The data usually are held with *relational database* software, which provides maximum flexibility and choice of analysis tools.

Interfaces, computer programs that grab the data from the source systems and restructure them into the components to go onto the marketing database. These programs are written by the in-house Information Technology (IT) staff, since they obtain and restructure data from the in-house sales records and other in-house systems.

Applications, the software programs that the planners use to analyze data and develop plans. Applications include data-grabbing tools that grab the items of data from their storage locations; reporting tools that summarize the data according to categories defined by the marketing department; and spreadsheets that carry out calculations and what-if analyses on the reported summary data. Applications also may include specific marketing-planning software, such as EXMAR, a decision support tool for strategic marketing planning. For further information on EXMAR, see the last page of this book.

The critical issue in building a system is that it is not self-contained within the marketing department. The system necessitates interface programs that alter the systems used by finance, sales, and other internal departments, as well as data feeds from external sources.

The secrets of success in developing systems for marketing are the following:

- Understanding what marketing needs and particularly how the internal and external views are to be reconciled
- Developing a strong cost-benefit case for information systems, given that other systems, including financial ones, have to be altered to accommodate the needs of marketing
- Working continuously with internal IT staff until the system is built. This department is under pressure from other sources, especially finance, and unless marketing maintains momentum and direction, other priorities will win.

Marketing planners need to become far less insular and parochial if they are to obtain the information they require to plan effectively. Cross-functional understanding and cooperation must be secured by the marketing department if it is to develop the systems it needs.

Forecasting

There are two major types of forecasting, which can be loosely described as *macroforecasting* and *microforecasting* (Figure 10-4). Selection of the appropriate technique depends on four main factors, the first of which is the degree of accuracy required. Second, the method depends on the availability of data and information. Third, the time horizon is a key determinant of the forecasting method. For example, are we forecasting sales for the next period, in which case quantitative extrapolative approaches may

Figure 10-4
Techniques of Forecasting: Quantitative and Qualitative

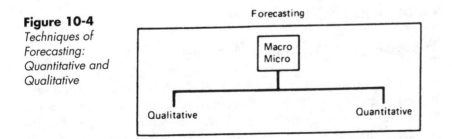

be appropriate, or are we forecasting what will happen to our principal market over the next five years, in which case qualitative approaches may be appropriate? Last, the position of the product in its life cycle is a key determinant of the forecasting method. For example, at the introductory stage of the life cycle of a product, fewer data and less information are available than at the maturity stage, when time series can be a useful forecasting method.

There is an important distinction between macro- and microforecasting. Macroforecasting entails the markets in total. Microforecasting is a detailed product unit forecast. Macroforecasting has to precede the establishment of marketing objectives and strategies. Detailed unit forecasts, or microforecasts, are made after the company has decided of which specific market opportunities it wants to take advantage and how best this can be done.

There are two major techniques for forecasting—*qualitative* and *quantitative*. It would be unusual if either of these methods were used entirely on its own, mainly because of the inherent dangers in each. Forecasters should combine an intuitive approach with a purely mathematical approach. For example, it is comparatively easy to develop an equation to extrapolate statistically the world population up to, say, the year 2010. The problem with such an approach is that it does not take into account likely changes in past trends. It would be easy to list a series of possible events that could affect world population and then assign probabilities to the likelihood of those events happening.

The task of management is to take the relevant data to help predict the future, to use on it whatever quantitative techniques are appropriate, and then to use qualitative methods such as expert opinion, market research, and analogy to predict the likely *discontinuities* in the time series. It is only through the sensible use of the available tools that management will begin to understand what has to be done to match its own capabilities with carefully selected market needs. Without such an understanding, any form of forecasting is likely to be a sterile exercise.

MARKETING ORGANIZATION

Organizing for Marketing Planning

The purpose of this section is not to delve into the complexities of organizational forms but to put the difficult process of marketing planning into the context of the environment in which it takes place. The point is that you start from where you *are*, not from where you would like to be. It is a fact of business that marketing means different things in different circumstances. It is not our intention to recommend any one particular organizational form. Our intention is to point out some of the more obvious organizational issues and their likely effect on the way marketing planning is conducted. As a result of the seemingly permanent debate surrounding organizational forms, we conducted a research study on the subject of marketing planning. The interesting fact that emerged was that most approaches to the subject concentrated almost exclusively on the "medicine" and showed relatively little concern for the "patient" (if indeed the company can be viewed as being ill and in need of attention). That makes about as much sense as a physician dispensing the same drug to every patient irrespective of his or her condition. The treatment might help a proportion of clients, but for a vast number it is at best irrelevant and at worst dangerous.

Organizational Life Phases

At first sight, every organization appears to be quite different from any other, and, of course, in many ways it is. Its personnel and facilities can never exist in the same form elsewhere. Its products, services, history, and folklore also play their part in creating a unique entity. Yet organizations also share similarities. As companies grow and mature, they *all* experience a number of distinct life phases. Our research has convinced us that once the phases of corporate life are explained to managers, the managers can readily position their own company on its lifeline. As firms grow in sales, they tend to go through an organizational evolution. When a firm starts business, it is often organized around the owner, who tends to know more about customers and products than anyone else in the company. This organizational form can be represented as in Figure 10-5, with all decisions and lines of communication revolving around one person. Formalized marketing planning by means of systems and written

Figure 10-5
The Wheel Organization

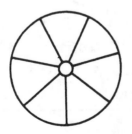

procedures is less relevant in this firm than in a diversified multinational company.

First stages of growth

As a firm grows in size and complexity, as new products and new markets are added, the wheel-like organizational form begins to break down and the first crisis appears, which is resolved in one of two ways. Either the owner-entrepreneur sells the business and retires or starts another business or he or she adopts an organizational structure in which certain functional duties are assigned to specialized departments. Systems and procedures are developed to replace the ad hoc arrangements of the initial phase. Above all, organizational loose ends have to be tied up and a new sense of purpose and direction instilled in the employees.

A strong leader is required to bring the company out of the leadership crisis phase and into the next, relatively calm period of directed evolution (Figure 10-6). Here, the leader, who may by now no longer be the founder, directs events from a centralized position. He or she presides over a hierarchical organizational structure which is set up to achieve what the leader prescribes. Again, steady growth can accompany this phase of corporate life until another crisis point is reached. This is the so-called autonomy crisis.

Eventually the company reaches a size or complexity at which the directive leadership is no longer appropriate. Individuals working in their particular spheres of activity know more than the central authority. They not only resent being told what to do by someone they perceive as out of touch but also want to have more personal autonomy to influence company policies and operations. The struggle for power during the autonomy crisis can be accompanied by a tightening of central control, which

Figure 10-6
*Organizational
Life Phases*

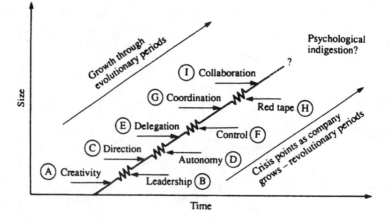

exacerbates the problem, causing poor morale and even, perhaps, high staff turnover.

The crisis is eventually resolved when the company provides a delegative style of leadership that generates more autonomy at lower levels. Again, a relatively trouble-free, evolutionary growth period follows from this delegative style. As growth continues, however, senior management becomes increasingly concerned about the high levels of autonomy lower down in the organization. Management feels powerless and senses the need to regain control. This control crisis can be another destabilizing phase in the development of a company. Understandable as the feelings of impotence might be for senior management, it is difficult to turn the clock back to a directive management style. Too much has happened in the intervening years.

The solution to the control crises is to embark on a program for establishing better coordination among the various parts of the organization. This is often achieved by using mechanisms such as formal planning procedures, centralization of some technical functions while leaving daily operating decisions at the local level, and setting up special projects involving lower-level employees. Another period of relative calm comes with the coordinated evolutionary phase of development.

With continued growth, there is a tendency for the coordinating practices to become institutionalized. Planning procedures become ritualized, special projects become meaningless chores, and too many decisions seem to be governed by company rules and regulations. A new crisis point has been reached—the bureaucracy or red-tape crisis. Procedures seem to take precedence over problem solving. The only solution seems to be for the company to strive toward a new phase of collaboration in which, once again, the contributions of individuals and teams are valued as much if not more than systems and procedures.

There has to be a concerted effort to re-energize and repersonalize operating procedures. More emphasis has to be put on teamwork, spontaneity, and creativity. If a company can win through to the collaborative phase of evolution, then, again, a period of relatively trouble-free growth can be expected as a reward. However, as we have seen, this pattern of evolutionary growth followed by a crisis appears to be ever-repeating. Each solution to an organizational development problem brings with it the seeds of the next crisis phase. The collaborative evolutionary crisis will probably end when there is a surfeit of integrating mechanisms and, perhaps, employees begin to lose the ability to function independently.

The last point is purely conjecture, because not many companies seem to have moved far enough along their biographic lifeline for this to be an issue. In the work we have completed in a number of companies, this idea of company life phases has helped us to understand much more about clients' operating problems and how we might provide help.

Second phase of growth

Within the second phase of growth, there are basically two kinds of organizations, which can be described as *decentralized* or *centralized*, with several combinations within each extreme. It is possible to represent decentralization as in Figure 10-7. The shaded area of the triangle represents the top-level strategic management of the firm. Central services, such as market research and public relations, are repeated at the subsidiary company level. There is a strategic level of management at the subsidiary level, the acid test being whether subsidiary company or unit top management can introduce new products without reference to headquarters.

Decentralized organizational structure leads inevitably to duplication of effort and overdifferentiation of strategies, with all the consequent problems, unless an effort is made to achieve some synergy among the several systems by means of a company-wide planning system.

One telecommunications equipment company had a range of 1500 products, and one of those products had 1300 variations, all of which was the result of a totally decentralized marketing-orientated approach in the subsidiary companies. Economies of scale in production were virtually impossible, with the result that the company operated at a substantial loss. The same problems apply to marketing research, advertising, pricing, distribution, and other business areas. For example, without coordination and oversight, the same market problem may be studied in many different countries around the world with no gain in market insight over what would have been found from one study. A decentralized organizational structure above all others necessitates strong central coordination by means of a planning system. Otherwise everyone wastes enormous amounts of corporate resources striving to maximize his or her own small part of the business.

Figure 10-7
Decentralization

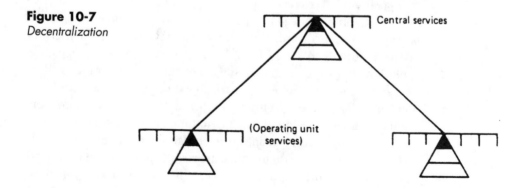

Central services

(Operating unit services)

If a system can be found to gain synergy from all the energy expended, the rewards are great. Marketing in this kind of system means something different from marketing in other kinds of systems. It is good to recognize this from the outset.

A centrally controlled company tends to look as depicted in Figure 10-8. There is no *strategic* level of management in the subsidiary units, particularly in respect to introduction of new products. This kind of organizational form tends to lead to standardized strategies, particularly in respect to product management. For example, when a new product is introduced, it tends to be designed at the outset with as many markets as possible in mind. The benefits from market research in one area are passed on to other areas.

The problem is that unless great care is exercised, subsidiary units can easily become insensitive to the needs of individual markets and lose flexibility in reacting to competitive moves.

We have looked briefly at two principal organizational forms, both of which consist essentially of a central office and various decentralized divisions, each with its own unique products, processes, and markets that complement the others in the group. In enterprises of this type, planning within the divisions applies to the exploration of markets and improved efficiency within the boundaries laid down by headquarters. The problems and opportunities that this method introduces tend to make the role of headquarters that of classifying the boundaries for the enterprise as a whole in relation to new products and markets that do not appear to fall within the scope of one of the divisions. In this type of organization, the managers of affiliated companies are required to produce the level of profit set by headquarters within the constraints imposed on them. Such companies need to institutionalize this process by providing a formal structure of ideas and systems so that operating management knows what it is expected to do and whether it is doing the essential things.

Figure 10-8
Centralization

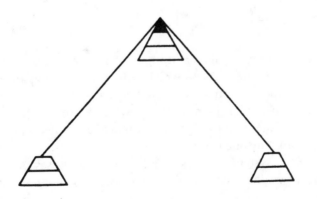

Organizing for Marketing

Before marketing planning systems are described, there are two additional points worth making about organizing for marketing. The first is that when marketing and sales are separated, marketing planning is going to be a different kind of activity from a situation in which both functions are coordinated at board level. In the first of these organizational forms, marketing is a staff activity, and the real power is vested in the sales organization. Although a strong chief executive can ensure that the two activities are sensibly coordinated, unfortunately this rarely happens because the executive is often too busy with production, distribution, personnel, and financial issues to devote enough time to sales and marketing. The point is that a sales force is quite correctly concerned with *today's* products, problems, and customers, whereas a marketing manager needs to be thinking about the *future*. The sales force is also quite correctly concerned mainly with *individual* products, problems, and customers, whereas a marketing manager needs to be thinking about groups of products and customers (portfolio management and market segmentation).

The two jobs are closely connected, but fundamentally different. Great care is necessary to ensure that what the marketing department is *planning* is the same as what the sales force is *doing* in the field. All too often they are not. The second kind of organizational form tends to make it easier to ensure a sensible coordination between planning and doing. (It should be noted here that this section owes much to the original work and thinking of Simon Majaro.)

The second point about marketing organizational forms is that *all* firms have to address the following issues:

- Functions (such as advertising, market research, and pricing)
- Products
- Markets
- Geographic locations
- Channels

Product managers or market managers? Most firms would readily agree that in most cases the two main issues are *products* and *markets*, which is why many companies have what are called product managers or market managers. There can be no right or wrong answer to the question of which of these is the better. Common sense dictates that market circumstances alone determine which is appropriate for any one company.

Each system has its strengths and weaknesses. A product manager–oriented system ensures strong product orientation, but can also easily lead to superficial market knowledge. Many a company has been caught when subtle changes in their several markets cause a product to become practically redundant. In consumer goods, for example, many companies are beginning to admit that their rigid product and brand management systems have allowed their more important customers to take the initiative. Many are now changing belatedly to a system in which the focus of marketing activity revolves around important customer and market groups rather than individual products. On the other hand, use of a market manager–orientated system can easily result in unnecessary product differentiation and poor *overall* product development. Whatever organizational form is adopted, the two central issues of products and markets constantly have to be addressed. This conundrum can be summarized in the following case study.

National Sealants, Inc., manufactures a range of adhesives that fall into two main categories—seals and sealants. The company supplies these products to a large number of markets. However, the main users come under four industry headings: gas, oil, and petrochemical refineries; automotive; electrical; and original equipment manufacturers (OEM). How should the marketing function be organized?

Figure 10-9 illustrates this case in what is often referred to as a *matrix* organization. Figure 10-10 puts this structure into the context of this particular company. Organizationally National Sealants has both a product management and market management structure. The basic role of the product manager is to ensure that the aspects of the product are properly managed. The role of the market manager is to pay particular attention to the needs of the market.

Figure 10-9
Products and Markets

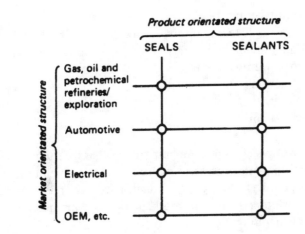

Figure 10-10
*Organization
of National
Sealants, Inc.*

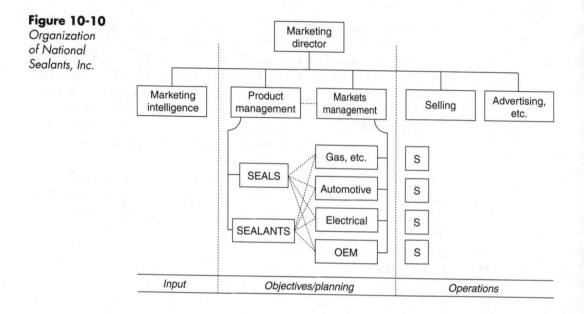

Close liaison between the two is necessary. A basic principle of this kind of organization is that authority for the final decision *must* be vested in either one or the other. Even when this is done, however, communication still can be difficult. Great care is necessary to ensure that vested interests are not allowed to dominate the real product and market issues.

To summarize, no one particular organizational form can be recommended. Common sense and market needs are the final arbiters. However, the following factors *always* have to be considered:

- Marketing centers of gravity
- Interface areas (e.g., present-future, sales force–design office)
- Authority and responsibility
- Ease of communication
- Coordination
- Flexibility
- Human factors

The world's leading companies now organize themselves around customer groups and processes, such as product development, rather than around products. Whenever practicable, we recommend organizing around customer groups, or markets, rather than around products, functions, or geography.

A Strategic Business Unit

- Has common segments and competitors for most of its products
- Is a competitor in an external market
- Is a discrete, separate, and identifiable unit
- Has a manager who has control over most of the areas critical to success

Strategic business units are not necessarily the same as operating units, and the definition can, and should, be applied all the way down to a particular product, or customer, or group of products or customers. It is here that the main marketing planning task lies.

One of the major determinants of the effectiveness of any marketing planning attempted within a company is the way that the company organizes for marketing. The purpose of this section is to point out some of the more obvious facts and pitfalls before we attempt to outline a marketing planning system, to which we turn in chapter 11.

The Marketing Planning Process and Corporate Culture

If marketing planning is acceptable at something deeper than a cosmetic level, it becomes possible to see how the process aligns with different phases of the company's lifeline.

Creative Evolution Phase

In our research, we did not find a single marketing planner at this stage of development. Most of the companies were still formulating their business ideas, and the senior executive (the culture carrier) was in close touch with customers and the company's own staff. The organization had a high level of flexibility to respond to changes in customer needs. In our research, many of these companies were showing high growth and to introduce marketing planning did not appear to offer any additional benefits.

If the company successfully negotiates this initial phase, eventually it reaches the leadership crisis. A strong leader is needed to provide the drive and direction to lead to the next evolutionary phase.

Two models, both directive, with differing impact

Directed Evolution

Companies at this stage of development fall into two camps. Naturally enough, the underlying style behind the marketing planning process is directive in each case, but the impact and effectiveness are different for each type.

The first type is *Directed Marketing Planning Type 1*. The senior executive takes responsibility or delegates the task of producing a marketing plan. This person then spends time analyzing data and performing a situational review until he or she finishes a document. An approval mechanism is built into the process. For example, the board of directors vets the marketing plan before it is issued, but thereafter the plan acts as a directive for the organization.

In *Directed Marketing Planning Type 2*, the appropriate members of the staff are told what information to provide about their areas of work and the form in which the information is to be provided. The plan is not directed; the process is spelled out carefully. The resulting information is assembled at a senior level, and the planning document is issued.

Although in both cases all the creative thinking and control take place at the top level of the organization, the second method is more likely to generate useful data without sacrificing the directive, power-based culture.

Delegated planning: an evolving process

Delegated Evolution

As a solution to the autonomy crisis that can develop when directive leadership becomes inappropriate, delegation becomes an operational feature of an organization. What seems to be a problem for marketing planning in these companies is that people in the front line, or operating units, of large companies are expected to produce marketing plans but without guidance. For example, one company had to send its marketing plans to the head office, where they were rigorously examined and then given the corporate thumbs up or thumbs down. Only through a process of acceptance or dismissal were the criteria for "good" plans eventually pieced together. Use of a delegated form of marketing planning can lead to some high-quality input and to high levels of commitment on behalf of those involved. Yet, ultimately, solely bottom-up planning procedures seem to be difficult to integrate and can be demotivating to those involved. Somehow the sum of the parts is less than it ought to be.

Coordinated Evolution

At the coordinated stage of evolution, the lessons of the directed and delegated phases seem to have been learned. There is more emphasis on a plan for planning and a means to incorporate top-down direction and bottom-up quality. A coordinated approach also enables the company to make the best use of its specialized resources and to generate commitment from the staff. However, it is possible for the planning process to degenerate from a problem-solving process into a fairly meaningless, bureaucratic ritual. It is at this stage that the planning process becomes counterproductive.

Collaborative Evolution

In collaborative evolution, the bureaucracy again has to make way for genuine problem solving. We do not have very much evidence about what this means in practice. It is possible to speculate that as business environments change at an ever-increasing pace, new marketing planning procedures might have to be developed. Creativity and expediency appear to be the passwords to this new phase of development.

This chapter shows how the acceptance of marketing planning is conditioned largely according to stage of development of the organization and behavior of the corporate culture carriers. Different modes of marketing planning became more appropriate at different phases of the company's life.

Marketing information is at the heart of a company's ability to plan. *Marketing research* is concerned with research into the entire marketing process. *Market research* is research about markets. Although the marketing planning process itself remains consistent throughout, *how* that process is managed must be congruent with the current organizational culture. The alternative is to take steps to change the company culture to make it amenable to a particular planning process. Because culture tends to act to maintain the existing power structure and the status quo, marketing planning interventions in companies must be recognized as having a political dimension and are not purely educational. Not least among the political issues is the question whether a company's management style can adapt sufficiently to enable the marketing planning process to deliver the rewards it promises.

QUESTIONS SUCCESSFUL COMPANIES ASK

1. Over what period of time do we forecast in our organization? Is it the right period? Do all relevant managers have an opportunity to make a contribution? If not, how can they become involved?
2. What influences whether research is conducted internally or by external consultants?
3. Is there ever a wide variance between forecasts and sales? If so, how do we explain it?
4. What additional information do we want to help us make accurate forecasts? How can we obtain such information? Why have we not obtained it in the past?
5. If we establish a new marketing information system for our company, what will it contain? How is it different from our current system and how can such a system be organized and made to work?

11

Implementation Issues in Marketing Planning

Chapter 11 opens with a discussion of the implications of size and diversity of operations in marketing planning. This is followed by a summary of the main elements of the marketing planning process. The roles of the chief executive and the planning department are discussed. That discussion is followed by some thoughts on the marketing planning cycle and planning horizons. Insights are provided into how the marketing planning process works.

An indication of the potential complexity of marketing planning is shown in Figure 11-1. Even a generalized model such as this shows that in a large, diversified group that operates in many foreign markets, a complex combination of product, market, and functional plans is possible. For example, what is required at the regional level is different from what is required at headquarters; it is clear, however, that the total corporate plan has to be built from the individual building blocks. Furthermore, the function of marketing itself may be further functionalized for the purpose of planning, such as marketing research, advertising, selling, distribution,

In chapter 3 we discussed some of the many myths that surround marketing planning and spelled out the conditions that must be satisfied if any company is to have an effective marketing planning system. These are:

1. Use of any closed-loop marketing planning system (but especially one that is essentially a forecasting and budgeting system) leads to entropy of marketing and creativity. Therefore, there has to be a mechanism to prevent inertia from setting in through overbureaucratization of the system.

2. Marketing planning undertaken at the functional level of marketing, in the absence of a means of integration with other functional areas of the business at general management level, is largely ineffective.

3. Separation of responsibility for operational and strategic marketing planning leads to a divergence of the short-term thrust of a business at the operational level from the long-term objectives of the enterprise as a whole. This encourages a preoccupation with short-term results at the operational level, which makes the firm less effective in the long term.

4. Unless the chief executive understands and takes an active role in marketing planning, the system will never be effective.

5. A period as long as three years is necessary, especially in large firms, for the successful introduction of an effective marketing planning system.

Figure 11-1
*Potential Complex-
ity of Marketing
Planning*

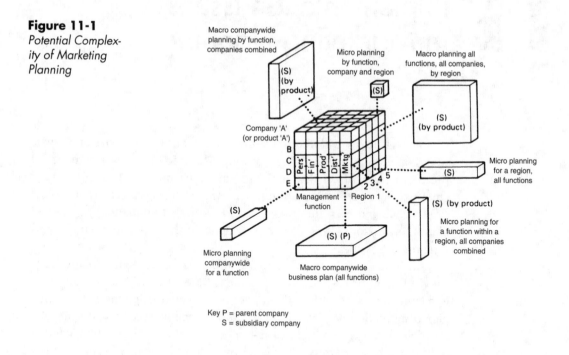

Key P = parent company
   S = subsidiary company

and promotion, while different customer groups may need to have separate plans.

Unnecessary planning, or overplanning, can easily result from inade-
quate or indiscriminate consideration of the real planning needs at the
different levels in the hierarchical chain. As size and diversity increase,
the degree of formalization of the marketing planning process must also
increase. This can be simplified in the form of a matrix (Figure 11-2). The
degree of formalization must increase with the evolving size and diversity
of operations. However, although the degree of formalization changes,
the need for a complete marketing planning system does not.

Central to the success of any enterprise is objective setting. Connected
with this is the question of the design of the planning system and, in particular, the questions of who is to be involved in what and how they are
to be involved. For example, who should perform the situation review,
state the assumptions, set marketing objectives and strategies, and conduct the scheduling and costing-out program and at what level? These
complex issues revolve essentially around two dimensions—the size of
the company and the degree of business diversity.

Figure 11-2
Degree of Formali-
zation of the
Marketing Plan-
ning Process:
Size and Diversity

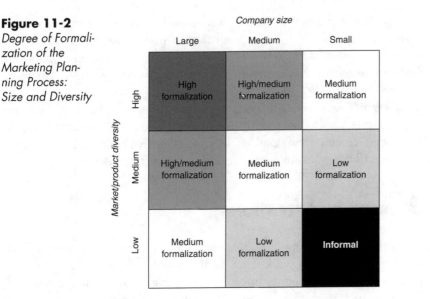

SIZE

Size of operations is, without doubt, the main determinant of the type of marketing planning system used. In small companies, there is rarely much diversity of products or markets, and top management has an in-depth knowledge of the key determinants of success and failure. There is usually a high level of knowledge of both technology and the market. Because in such companies the central control mechanism is the sales forecast and budget, top managers are able to explain the rationale behind the numbers, have a very clear view of their comparative strengths and weaknesses, and are able to explain the company's marketing strategy without difficulty. Understanding and familiarity with the strategy are shared with key operating subordinates by means of personal, face-to-face dialogue throughout the year. Subordinates operate within a logical framework of ideas, which they understand. There is a shared understanding between top and middle management of the industry and prevailing business conditions. Such companies, therefore, operate according to a set of structured procedures and complete the several steps in the marketing planning process but in a relatively informal manner.

Size determines planning systems.
On the other hand, many small companies that have a poor understanding of the marketing concept, and in which the top manager leaves the strategy implicit, suffer many serious operational problems. These operational problems become progressively worse as the size of company in-

179

creases. As the number of managers and levels of management increase, it becomes progressively more difficult for top management to enjoy an in-depth knowledge of industry and business conditions acquired by informal, face-to-face means. In the absence of written procedures and a structured framework, the different levels of operating management become increasingly less able to react in a rational way to pressures. Systems of tight budgeting control, without the procedures outlined in this book, are successful only in buoyant trading conditions, are often the cause of high levels of management frustration, and are seen to contribute to eventual decline.

DIVERSITY OF OPERATIONS

From the point of view of management control, the least complex environment in which to work is an undiversified company, that is, a company with limited product lines or homogeneous customer groups. For example, hydraulic hose can be sold to many diverse markets, or a diverse range of products can be sold into only one market, such as the automotive industry. Both companies can be classified as undiversified.

In undiversified companies, the need for institutionalized marketing planning systems increases with the size of the operation, and there is a strong relation between size and the complexity of the management task, irrespective of apparent diversity. For example, an oil company operates in many diverse markets around the world, through many different kinds of marketing systems, and with varying levels of market growth and market share. In most respects, therefore, the control function for head-quarters management is just as difficult and complex as that in a large, diversified conglomerate. The main difference is the greater level of in-depth knowledge that top management has about the key determinants of success and failure underlying the product or market worldwide, because of its homogeneity. Because of this homogeneity of product or market, it is usually possible for headquarters to impose worldwide policies on operating units in respect to factors such as certain aspects of advertising, public relations, packaging, pricing, trademarks, and product development. At the headquarters of a diversified conglomerate, overall policies are impractical. To summarize, the smaller the company, the more informal and personal are the procedures for marketing planning. As company size and diversity increase, the need for more formalized procedures increases.

Companies that conform to the framework outlined herein have systems that, through a hierarchy of bottom up–top down negotiating procedures, reach a balance between the need for detailed control at the lowest level of operations and centralized control. The main role of headquarters is to harness the company's strengths on a worldwide basis and to ensure that lower level decisions do not cause problems in other areas and lead to wasteful duplication.

Figure 11-3 shows four key outcomes that marketing planning can evoke. Systems II, III, and IV, in which individuals are totally subordinate to a formalized system, individuals are allowed to do what they want without any system, or there is neither system nor creativity, are less successful than system I, in which the individual is allowed to be entrepreneurial within a total system. System I, then, is an effective marketing planning system but one in which the degree of formalization is a function of company size and diversity.

Creativity cannot flourish in a closed-loop formalized system. There would be little disagreement that in today's abrasive, turbulent, and highly competitive environment, the firms that will succeed in the long run are those that succeed in extracting entrepreneurial ideas and creative marketing programs from systems that are necessarily yet acceptably formalized. Much innovative flair can easily become stifled by systems.

There is ample evidence of international companies with highly formalized systems that produce stale and repetitive plans in which little is changed from year to year and that fail to point out the key strategic is-

Any closed-loop planning system, especially if based on forecasting and budgeting alone, deadens creative response and eventually leads to failure.

Figure 11-3
Four Types of Marketing Planning

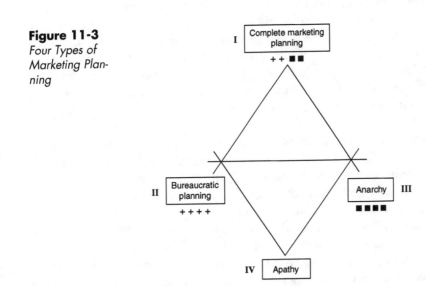

+ Degree of formalization
■ Degree of openness

sues. The waste this implies is largely due to a *lack of personal intervention by key managers during the early stages of the planning cycle*. There is a need, therefore, to find a way of perpetually renewing the planning life cycle each time around. Inertia must never set in. Without a valve or means of opening the loop, inertia quickly produces decay. The critical intervention of senior managers, from the chief executive down through the hierarchical chain, comes at the audit stage. Such a valve has to be inserted early in the planning cycle during the audit or situation review stage. What takes place essentially is a personalized presentation of audit findings with proposed marketing objectives and strategies and outline budgets for the strategic planning period. These are discussed, amended where necessary, and agreed in various synthesized formats at the hierarchical levels in the organization *before* any detailed operational planning takes place. It is at such meetings that managers are called upon to justify their views, which tends to force them to be more bold and creative than they would have been had they been allowed merely to send in their proposals. Even in this situation much depends on the degree to which managers take a critical stance, which is much greater when the chief executive takes an active part in the process. *Every hour of time the chief executive devotes at this stage has a multiplier effect throughout the remainder of the process.*

Until recently it was believed that there may be fundamental differences in marketing planning approaches depending on factors such as the types of industrial goods and markets involved, company size, the degree of dependence on overseas sales, and the methods used to market goods abroad. In particular, the much debated role of headquarters management in the marketing planning process is frequently put forward as being a potential cause of great difficulty. One of the most encouraging findings to emerge from our research is that the theory of marketing planning is universally applicable and that the factors mentioned above are largely irrelevant.

Although planning is less complicated in small, undiversified companies and there is less need for formalized procedures than in large, diversified companies, the fact is that exactly the same framework is used in all circumstances. This approach brings similar benefits to all.

In a global company headquarters, management can assess trends in products and markets around the world and is able to develop strategies on a global basis. Subsidiary management can develop appropriate national strategies that address national market and competitive realities. This is achieved by means of synthesized information flows from the bottom upward, which facilitates useful comparison of performance around the world, and the diffusion of valuable information, skills, experiences, and systems from the top downward. The benefits that accrue to companies that use such systems can be classified under the headings of the marketing mix elements, as follows:

Marketing information There is a transfer of knowledge, a sharing of expertise and an optimization of effort around the world.

Product Control is exercised over the product range. Maximum effectiveness is gained by concentrating on certain products in certain markets on the basis of experience gained throughout the world.

Price Pricing policies are sufficiently flexible to enable local management to compete effectively without creation of a gray market for the company's products.

Place Substantial gains are made by means of rationalization of the logistics function.

Promotion Duplication of effort and a multitude of different platforms and company images are ameliorated. Efforts in one part of the world reinforce those in another.

The procedures that facilitate the provision of such information and knowledge transfer also encourage operational management to think strategically about its own areas of responsibility, instead of managing only for the short term.

SUMMARY OF THE MARKETING PLANNING PROCESS

The purpose of this section is to summarize earlier chapters and to ensure that the many threads developed are seen in their correct context within the marketing planning process.

It is good to remember above all else that the *purpose* of marketing planning is to create value for customers and competitive advantage for the firm. The following subsections identify the main barriers to marketing planning, summarize the main elements of a marketing planning system, and provide the basis for the design of a system suitable for any business.

The Process Itself

How well should we be doing in present market conditions? The answer to this question requires considerable analysis inside and outside the company. Simply looking at the bottom line and saying "budget achieved" is not enough. It is quite possible to achieve budget and still lose market share if the budget is not developed from a proper qualitative assessment of the market in the first place.

The real question to ask is, *What sales and gross profits should we be achieving in current market conditions?* To answer this and the previous question, it is necessary to have available a well-argued common format in the organization, that is, a marketing plan.

Undertaking marketing planning is a messy process that evolves over time. In effect, you are attempting to influence future outcomes by deciding *what to do about the possible different marketing environments.* In undertaking marketing planning, you join the ranks of those who make things happen in the company. The alternative is to be tossed around like a cork in the sea of competition. The planning process facilitates and depends on interactive communication up and down the organization. If this communication does not occur, all that results are forecasts projected from history rather than development of genuine objectives based on what is actually happening inside and outside the company.

Once the marketing planning process has developed through to the agreement of a detailed one-year operational plan, and once this budget is agreed, commitment must be total. If during the course of the ensuing fiscal year, performance begins to fall behind the budget or new opportunities appear, any part of the plan can and should be modified. There is flexibility in the way the elements of a plan can be altered and manipulated; the budget normally remains fixed. If key facts or assumptions on which the plan is based turned out to be in error, it may be necessary to change the budget.

The Marketing Audit

The marketing planning process starts with an *audit* of the company's operating performance and environment. The marketing audit is essentially a *database* of all market-related issues with which the company is concerned. The subsequent SWOT (strengths, weaknesses, opportunities, and threats) analysis lends structure to the audit to facilitate ongoing planning activities.

The company must provide a list of detailed questions that each manager is required to consider for his or her own area of responsibility. Each manager conducting an audit uses sales data and the company marketing information system to complete the audit. If the company has a marketing research manager, it is helpful at this stage to issue to all managers a market overview that covers important market and product trends.

Managers should create a product and market bible to use throughout the year.

It will probably be necessary to customize the audit checklist contents according to the level in the organization to which the audit is addressed. In this way, each particular checklist is made meaningful and relevant to each level. Some brief explanatory definitions also may be necessary. The audit inevitably requires more data preparation than is finally reproduced in the marketing plan. Managers should create a product and market bible or fact book to organize audit data for reference and easy access. The marketing audit is conducted on a *continuing* (dynamic) basis rather than at a particular point in time. In this way, it becomes a useful information source to draw on for decision making throughout the year.

Do not try to hide behind vague items in the audit, such as "poor economic condition." Even in overall static or declining markets growth points are present. Seek these out and decide whether or not to concentrate your efforts on them. The audit can be a useful transfer when new managers or executives take over a job. The incoming manager can quickly understand the business, and the organizational memory is not erased by the job.

SWOT Analysis

It is only the SWOT analysis, *not* the audit, that actually appears in the marketing plan. This summary of the audit if possible contains not more than four or five pages of commentary focusing on *key* factors only. It lists internal *differential* strengths and weaknesses in relation to competitors and key external opportunities and threats. A SWOT analysis is completed for each segment or product considered to be crucial to the future of the firm.

A SWOT analysis is interesting to read, contains concise statements, includes only relevant and important data, and gives greater emphasis to creative analysis. A crucial task for marketing management is to differentiate a company from its competitors. The SWOT analysis assists you in that task. A SWOT analysis well done helps to identify the real issues to be addressed in the future as a matter of priority. Too often, however, the SWOT summary is simply a smorgasbord of apparently unrelated points (in which case any underlying theme is difficult to discern). After listening to someone presenting a SWOT summary, you should end up with a clear understanding of the main thrust of their business. The SWOT statement encapsulates your perception of the marketplace, summarizes what you are trying to do, and points toward required future actions. The SWOT analysis is, by definition, a summary of the key issues emanating from the marketing audit. A SWOT analysis answers the following questions:

- What are the key trends that will affect our business?
- What do customers need?
- What do customers want?
- How do customers buy?
- What do our competitors offer?
- What are our competitors' plans and intentions?

Strengths and weaknesses

A SWOT analysis, to be effective and useful, must be differential. This is especially true of the strengths and weaknesses part of the analysis. *Differential* means the analysis must show a difference. Most SWOT analyses are merely a list of baseline capabilities and are therefore useless as the basis for strategic planning. Baseline capabilities are not strengths. They are the price of admission to an industry. Strengths are differential advantages. For example, for Saturn the dealer organization is clearly a strength. Saturn dealers deliver a level of service that is exceptional for the industry. The dealer organization is a differential advantage for Saturn and clearly belongs in the SWOT analysis. Weaknesses may be, and typically are, the absence of baseline capabilities. For example, before Harley Davidson started shamelessly copying Japanese motorcycle manufacturers, the company's product quality was a serious weakness in relation to the competition.

Opportunities and threats

For the opportunities and threats part of a SWOT analysis, the focus should be on identifying macro- and micro-opportunities and threats. Macro-opportunities and macrothreats include those that come from economic, technological, social, cultural, and political change. For example, in globalizing industries, a macrothreat is posed by competition from lower wage countries. Micro-opportunities and microthreats come from markets and customers and from existing and new direct and indirect competitors.

Companies in the information industry face a bewildering set of SWOT forces as government regulation changes the rules and boundaries of competition, new technologies emerge, and customers and markets rapidly change in response to the variety of new offerings. Everything is moving, and no amount of SWOT analysis will stop the dynamic evolution of markets and industries. SWOT analysis, however, does provide the basis for a deeper understanding of what to do to better serve customers and achieve greater competitive advantage.

Finally, agreed budgets (which come at the end of the process) must reflect internal consistency with the issues raised in the original SWOT analysis. Often this internal consistency is not evident, because budgets are written first rather than last, and the qualitative content is established last rather than first (in which case it is simply rhetoric). It is difficult to work with a SWOT analysis prepared by another person, unless you are involved in the original debate. The quality of a SWOT analysis will suffer under the following circumstances:

- It does not identify the critical issues, key strengths and weaknesses, and main opportunities and threats.
- It is too long and detailed.
- It is too short and cryptic.

It is great self-discipline to complete a good, tight, but comprehensive SWOT analysis.

Assumptions

Assumptions appear in the marketing plan. List the main assumptions on which the plan is based. If the plan can be implemented irrespective of any assumption made, then the assumption is unnecessary. Assumptions should be few in number and key.

Marketing Objectives

Marketing objectives appear in the marketing plan. Marketing objectives are about products and markets only (*not* about advertising). Marketing objectives flow from the SWOT analysis and are fully compatible with the key issues identified in the SWOT analysis. Marketing objectives are quantifiable and measurable for performance-monitoring purposes. Avoid directional terms such as "improve," "increase," and "expand." There are a hierarchy of marketing objectives down through the organization. Try to set priorities for your chosen marketing objectives.

Many so-called marketing objectives are in fact really marketing strategies—do not confuse the two. Marketing objectives are *what* we want to achieve; marketing strategies are *how* we intend to achieve the objectives.

In some cases, marketing strategies and detailed marketing *actions* are confused. Actions are the short-term list of activities performed according to a schedule that in aggregate amount to a particular strategy.

Marketing Strategies

Marketing strategies must appear in the marketing plan. Strategies are how the objectives are to be achieved, as follows:

- *Product* policies that include elements such as functions, design, size, and packaging
- *Pricing* policies to be followed for product groups in market segments
- *Place* policies for channels and customer service levels
- *Promotion* policies for communicating with customers under the relevant headings such as advertising, personal selling, and sales promotion

Programs

Detailed programs (sometimes called *appropriation budgets*) appear only in the detailed one-year operational marketing plan. In a three-year strategic marketing plan, all that is required are the financial implications (budget) of the agreed strategies. In a detailed one-year marketing plan, specific sub-objectives for products and segments are supported by detailed strategy and action statements, such as what, where, when, and costs. Include *budgets* and *forecasts* and a *consolidated budget*. The preparation of budgets and sales forecasts *must* reflect the marketing objectives. The objectives, strategies, and programs *must* reflect the agreed budgets and sales forecasts.

Forecasts (in lieu of objectives) are nothing more than an extrapolation of past experience. The marketing plan takes a zero-based view of current and possible future environments to arrive at a viable set of objectives. Unit forecasts follow. This is necessary to identify possible discontinuities in the future trading environment. Simple extrapolation of historical data ignores the possibility that discontinuities can (and do) occur.

A deep perception of the marketplace is needed to review and reveal viable marketing objectives and strategies, which are consistent with the company's distinctive competence. Individual budget items must clearly be traceable to issues identified in the original SWOT analysis. When measuring performance, at all times seek to relate to the outside market as well as to your internal budget.

The Written Marketing Plan

A written marketing plan (or plans) is the outcome of the marketing planning process. It is a business proposition that contains proposed courses of action, which have resource implications. Written marketing plans verbalize (and formalize) the intuitive model of the market environment within which you operate. Written marketing plans help to make things happen. The acid test of any marketing plan presentation is to ask yourself, Would I put my own life savings into the plan as presented? If the answer is no, then further work is needed to refine your ideas.

Good discipline in preparing internally consistent marketing plans is to use the following summary formula:

SWOT issues → Objectives → Strategy → Specific actions and timing

Role of the Chief Executive in Marketing Planning

Marketing planning that is not integrated with other functional areas of the business at the general management level is largely ineffective.

Our research has revealed that many chief executive officers (CEOs) do not have a clear understanding of the following:

- Purposes and methods of planning
- Proper assignments of planning responsibilities throughout the organization
- Proper structures and staffing of the planning department
- The talent and skills required in an effective planning department

The role of the CEO in marketing planning is critical: it is nothing less than to act as a catalyst for the entrepreneurial creativity that is inherent in every organization. Jack Welch, chairman and CEO of General Electric and a model of the CEO as catalyst calls this *delayering.*

Jack Welch Describes Delayering at General Electric

While we were restructuring the businesses, we also changed the management hardware at GE. We delayered. We removed sectors, groups, strategic business units and much of the extensive command structure and staff apparatus we used to run the company.

We cleared out stifling bureaucracy, along with the strategic planning apparatus, corporate staff empires, rituals, endless studies and briefings, and all the classic machinery that makes big-company operations smooth and predictable—but often glacially slow. As the underbrush of bureaucracy was cleared away, we began to see and talk to each other more clearly and more directly.

(Source: Annual Report, General Electric Company, 1995, p. 2.)

THE MARKETING PLANNING CYCLE

The schedule calls for work on the plan for the next year to begin early enough in the current year to allow adequate time for market research and analysis of key data and market trends. In addition, the plan provides for early development of a strategic plan that can be approved or altered in principle.

A key factor in determining the planning cycle is the degree to which it is practical to extrapolate from sales and market data. In general, however, companies that plan successfully start the formal planning cycle nine to six months from the beginning of the next fiscal year.

PLANNING HORIZONS

One- and five-year planning periods are common, although three years has become the most common period for the strategic plan, largely because of the dramatically increasing rate of environmental change. Lead time for the initiation of important product innovations, the length of time necessary to recover capital investment costs, the continuing availability of customers and raw materials, and the size and usefulness of existing plant and buildings are the most frequently mentioned reasons for having a five-year planning horizon. Increasingly, however, these five-year plans are taking the form more of scenarios than the detailed strategic plan described in this book.

Many companies do not give sufficient thought to the planning horizon for their particular circumstances. A five-year time span is clearly too long for some companies, particularly those operating in volatile fashion-conscious markets. On the other hand, for companies in industries that require long-term capital commitments, five years may be far too short a horizon. Each company must select the appropriate planning horizon.

HOW THE MARKETING PLANNING PROCESS WORKS

One other aspect to be considered concerns the location of the marketing planning activity in a company. The answer is simple. Marketing planning should take place as close to the marketplace as possible. Because in all but the smallest of undiversified companies it is not possible for top management to set detailed objectives for operating units, it is suggested that at this stage in the planning process, strategic guidelines be issued. One way of doing this is in the form of a *strategic planning letter* (Table 11-1).

TABLE 11-1 Chief Executive's Strategic Planning Letter (Possible Areas for Which Objective and Strategies or Strategic Guidelines Will Be Set)

Financial	*Operations*
Remittances	Land
Dividends	Buildings
Royalties	Plant
Gross margin %	Modifications
Operating profit	Maintenance
Return on capital employed	Systems
Debtors	Raw materials
Creditors	Supplies
Bank loans	Purchasing
Investments	Distribution
Capital expenditure	Stock and control
Cash flow controls	Transportation
	Warehousing
Human resources and organization	*Marketing*
Management	Target markets
Training	Market segments
Industrial relations	Brands
Organization	Volumes
Remuneration and pensions	Market shares
	Pricing
	Image
	Promotion
	Market research
	Quality control
	Customer service

Another is by means of a personal briefing by the CEO at kick-off meetings.

The interdependence between the top-down and bottom-up processes is illustrated in Figures 11-4 and 11-5, which show a hierarchy in respect to objective and strategy setting similar to that illustrated in respect to audits.

Figure 11-4
*Top-Down and
Bottom-Up*

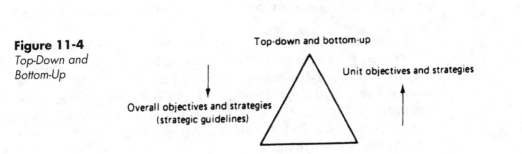

Figure 11-5
*Strategic and
Operational
Planning*

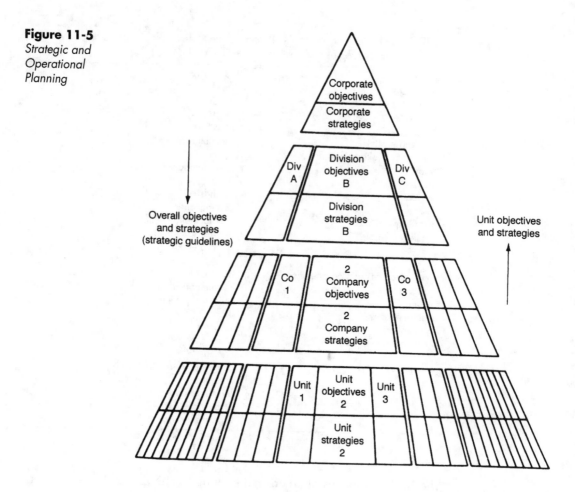

Having shown the point about *requisite* marketing planning, these figures also illustrate the principles by which the marketing planning process should be implemented in any company, irrespective of whether it is a small company or a large multinational firm. In essence, these exhibits show a *hierarchy* of audits, SWOT analyses, objectives, strategies, and programs.

Figure 11-6 is another way of illustrating the total corporate strategic and planning process. In Figure 11-6, however, a time element is added, and the relation between strategic planning letters, long-term corporate plans, and short-term operational plans is clarified. There are two open loop points in Figure 11-6. These are the key times in the planning process when a subordinate's views and findings are subjected to the closest examination by a superior.

Figure 11-6
Total Corporate Strategic and Planning Process

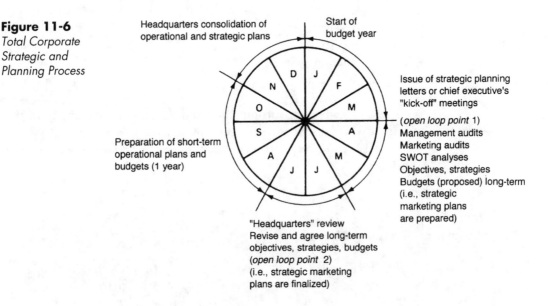

FINAL THOUGHT

There is no such thing as a ready-made marketing planning system. Nonetheless, our research and experience indicate that marketing planning remains a great bastion of management ignorance, largely because of the complexity of the process and its organizational, political, and cultural implications.

Chapter 12 summarizes the main points described in the book and provides a simple, step-by-step system that can become the basis of planning procedures. The system has been used successfully in businesses ranging from large international industrial companies to small domestic service organizations.

Success comes from *experience*. Experience comes from making mistakes. We can minimize these if we combine *common sense* and *sweet reasonableness* with the models provided in this book. But be sure of one thing: The models do not work by themselves. If you read this book carefully and use the models sensibly, marketing planning becomes one of the most powerful tools available to a business today. It can take three years to introduce marketing planning successfully. The correct planning horizon differs from firm to firm, depending on the business. Small firms can use shorter horizons, because they are flexible, to adjust to change. Large firms need longer horizons.

Companies often set out to achieve the impossible. It is not unknown to see planning objectives which seek to do the following:

- Maximize sales
- Minimize costs
- Increase market share
- Maximize profits

These objective are incompatible and damage the credibility of the managers who subscribe to such commitments.

We wish you every success in your endeavors and leave you with ten principles.

Ten Principles of Marketing Planning

1. Develop the strategic plan first; the operational plan should be guided by a strategic plan.
2. Put marketing as close as possible to the customer and make marketing and sales the responsibility of one person.
3. See marketing as an attitude of mind, not merely a set of procedures.
4. Organize activities around customer groups, not functional activities.
5. Make your marketing audit rigorous. Allow no vague terms, and hide nothing. Use tools such as portfolio analysis and product life cycle.
6. Focus SWOT analyses on segments that are critical to the business; concentrate only on key factors that lead to your objectives.
7. Educate people about the planning process.
8. Plan your planning.
9. Prioritize objectives in terms of their urgency and impact.
10. Enlist the active support of all organization members, from the CEO to the telephone receptionist, and make sure the entire organization is enrolled in the plan.

12 A Step-by-Step Marketing Planning System

This chapter is divided into two parts. The first is a summary of the main points related to marketing planning. The second part is an actual marketing planning system that puts into operation all the concepts, structures, and frameworks outlined in this book in the form of a step-by-step approach to the preparation, first, of a strategic and, second, of an operational marketing plan.

SUMMARY OF MARKETING PLANNING

Marketing planning is the process that leads to the creation of a marketing plan. The marketing plan is a systematic design for achieving the objectives of creating value for customers and of competitive advantage, growth, and profitability for the organization. The preparation of a marketing plan requires an in-depth analysis of the market and competitive situation, the formulation of a marketing strategy and action programs, and the preparation of pro-forma income and other financial statements. Marketing planning is essential for any organization that wants to achieve the full potential of market opportunities.

Ten Barriers to Marketing Planning

1. Confusion between marketing tactics and strategy
2. Isolation of the marketing function from operations
3. Confusion between the marketing function and the marketing concept
4. Organizational barriers—too many business layers
5. Lack of in-depth analysis
6. Confusion between process and output
7. Lack of knowledge and skills
8. Lack of a systematic approach to marketing planning
9. Failure to prioritize objectives
10. Hostile corporate cultures

The Ten S's to Overcoming Barriers to Achieve Superior Performance

Strategy before tactics
Situate marketing within operations
Shared values about marketing
Structure around markets
Scan the environment

Summarize information in SWOT (strengths, weaknesses, opportunities, and threats) analyses
Skills and knowledge
Systematize the process
Sequence objectives
Style and culture

The Principles

Principle 1: Strategy Before Tactics

Develop the strategic marketing plan first. This entails emphasis on scanning the external environment, identifying early forces emanating from it, and developing appropriate strategic responses. Involve all levels of management in the process. A strategic plan covers a period of three to five years. Only when this plan has been developed and agreed upon is a one-year operational marketing plan developed. *Never* write the one-year plan first and extrapolate it.

Principle 2: Situate Marketing Within Operations

For the purpose of marketing planning, put marketing as close as possible to the customer. When practical, have both marketing and sales report to the same person, who is not the chief executive officer.

Principle 3: Shared Values About Marketing

Marketing is a management process whereby the resources of the entire organization are used to satisfy the needs of selected customer groups to achieve the objectives of both parties. Marketing is an attitude of mind rather than a series of functional activities.

Principle 4: Structure Around Markets

Organize company activities around customer groups if possible rather than around functional activities, and conduct marketing planning done in these strategic business units. Without excellent marketing planning in strategic business units, corporate marketing planning is of limited value.

Principle 5: Scan the Environment Thoroughly

The following are requirements for an effective marketing audit:

Checklists of questions customized according to level in the organization are prepared.

The checklists form the basis of the organization's Marketing Information System (MIS).

The marketing audit is a *required* activity.

Managers are not allowed to hide behind vague terms, such as "poor economic conditions."

Managers are encouraged to incorporate the tools of marketing in their audits, such as product life cycles and portfolios.

Principle 6: Summarize Information in SWOT Analyses

Information is the foundation on which a marketing plan is built. From information (internal and external) comes intelligence. A SWOT analysis does the following:

Focuses on each specific segment of crucial importance to the organization's future

Is a summary emanating from the marketing audit

Is brief, interesting, and concise

Focuses on *key* factors only

Lists *differential* strengths and weaknesses in relation to competitors, focusing on competitive advantage

Lists *key* external opportunities and threats only

Identifies the *real* issues, is not a list of unrelated points

Is clear enough for a reader to grasp instantly the main thrust of the business, even to the point of being able to write marketing objectives

Answers the implied question "which means that . . . ?" to get the real implications

Does not leave out important facts, questions, and issues.

Principle 7: Skills and Knowledge

Ensure that all those responsible for marketing have the necessary marketing knowledge and skills for the job. In particular, ensure that they understand and know how to use the tools of marketing, such as the following:

Information and scanning

Positioning

Market segmentation

Targeting

Product life cycle analysis

Portfolio management

Gap analysis

Boston Consulting Group matrix

Directional policy matrix

Four Ps of management—product, price, place, promotion

Marketing personnel also need communication and interpersonal skills.

Principle 8: Systematize the Process

It is essential to have a set of written procedures and a well-argued common format for marketing planning. The purposes of such a system are as follows:

1. To ensure that all key issues are systematically considered
2. To pull together the essential elements of the strategic plan in a consistent manner
3. In a multibusiness enterprise, to help corporate management to compare diverse businesses and to understand the overall condition of and prospects for the organization.

Principle 9: Sequence Objectives

Ensure that all objectives are prioritized according to their impact on the organization and their urgency and that resources are allocated accordingly.

Principle 10: Style and Culture

Marketing planning is not effective without the active support and participation of top management. But even with this support, the type of marketing planning has to be appropriate for the phase of the organizational lifeline. This phase is measured before an attempt is made to introduce marketing planning.

Conclusion

Marketing planning never has been the simple step-by-step approach described so enthusiastically in most prescriptive texts and courses. The moment an organization embarks on the marketing planning path, it can expect to encounter a number of complex organizational, attitudinal, process, and strategic issues. If you are aware of these barriers, you are much more likely to be successful using the step-by-step marketing planning system described in the following section. Figure 12-1 summarizes the marketing planning process.

Part 2: A Marketing Planning System

A MARKETING PLANNING SYSTEM

The marketing planning system is divided into two sections. Section A takes you through a step-by-step approach to the preparation of a strategic marketing plan. Section B provides instruction about the content of a strategic marketing plan.

Section A: A Step-by-Step Approach to the Preparation of a Strategic Marketing Plan

There are four steps in the planning process:

1. **Analysis** The business must analyze the market, the broader business environment, the competition, and its position relative to the competition.
2. **Objectives** The business must set, based on analysis, a realistic set of quantitative marketing and financial objectives.
3. **Strategy** The business must determine the broad strategy to accomplish these objectives.
4. **Tactics** The business must draw together the analysis, the objectives, and the strategy and use them as the foundation for detailed tactical action plans that will implement the strategy and achieve the company's objectives.

This process is formally expressed in two plans, the strategic and the tactical marketing plan. It is designed to enable business units to be able to

Figure 12-1 *A Summary of the Marketing Planning Process*

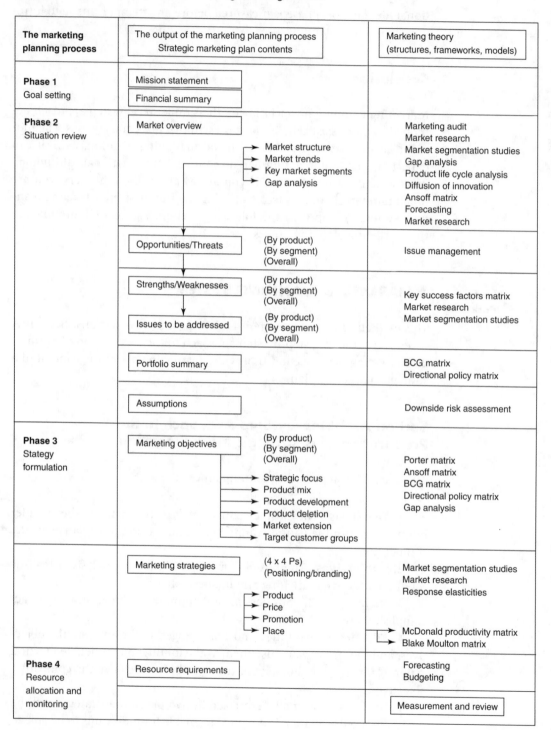

take a logical and constructive approach to planning for success. The following two important points should be made about the marketing plan.

The Importance of Different Sections

In the final analysis, the strategic marketing plan is a plan for action, and this should be reflected in the finished document. The implementation part of the strategic plan is represented by the subsequent one-year marketing plan.

The Length of the Analytical Section

For an action-focused strategic marketing plan, a considerable amount of background information and data must be collected and analyzed. An analytical framework is provided in the forms included in the database section of the document. The commentary in the strategic marketing plan should provide the main findings of analysis rather than a mass of raw data. It compels concentration on only that which is essential. The analysis section therefore provides only a brief background.

The following sections explain how each of the steps in the planning process is to be completed. For the sake of simplicity, it has been assumed that the organization's year runs from January to December. Figure 12-2 outlines the marketing planning process.

The Marketing Audit

Marketing audit data are *not included in the marketing plan* or its presentation. The marketing audit requires more data than are needed for reproduction in the marketing plan itself. Therefore, all managers should start a *running reference file* for their area of responsibility during the year. This file also can be used as a continual reference source and for presentation of proposals.

Contents of a Strategic Marketing Plan

Sections 1 through 9 describe the content of a strategic marketing plan. These steps are completed by the end of May each year. These sections contain instructions. The actual documentation for the strategic marketing plan is also provided in this section.

Figure 12-2
An Outline of the Marketing Planning Process

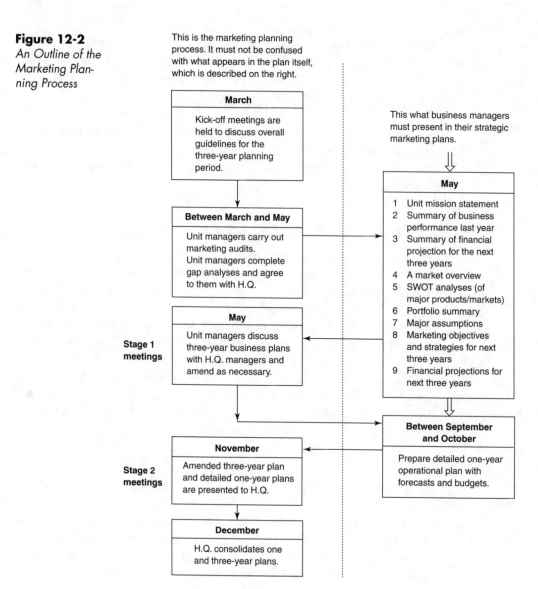

This is the marketing planning process. It must not be confused with what appears in the plan itself, which is described on the right.

March

Kick-off meetings are held to discuss overall guidelines for the three-year planning period.

Between March and May

Unit managers carry out marketing audits.
Unit managers complete gap analyses and agree to them with H.Q.

May

Unit managers discuss three-year business plans with H.Q. managers and amend as necessary.

Stage 1 meetings

This what business managers must present in their strategic marketing plans.

May

1 Unit mission statement
2 Summary of business performance last year
3 Summary of financial projection for the next three years
4 A market overview
5 SWOT analyses (of major products/markets)
6 Portfolio summary
7 Major assumptions
8 Marketing objectives and strategies for next three years
9 Financial projections for next three years

Between September and October

Prepare detailed one-year operational plan with forecasts and budgets.

November

Stage 2 meetings

Amended three-year plan and detailed one-year plans are presented to H.Q.

December

H.Q. consolidates one and three-year plans.

1. Mission Statement

The mission statement is the first item to appear in the marketing plan. The purpose of the mission statement is to ensure that the raison d'être of the business is clearly stated. Brief statements should be made that cover the following points:

- Role or contribution of the unit, such as profit generator, service department, opportunity seeker

- Definition of business, such as the needs you satisfy or the benefits you provide. Avoid being too specific (e.g., "we sell recorded music") or too general (e.g., "we are in the entertainment business").
- Distinctive competence. This should be a brief statement that applies only to your business. A statement that applies equally to any competitor is unsatisfactory.
- Indications for future direction—a brief statement of the principal things to which you give serious consideration (e.g., moving into a new segment). A statement about what you *will* consider, *might* consider, and *will never* consider can be quite useful.

2. Summary of Performance

This summary is designed to give a bird's eye view of total marketing activity. In addition to a financial summary of performance, as shown in Table 12-1, managers should give a summary of reasons for good or bad performance.

3. Summary of Financial Projections

The aim of the summary of financial projections is to enable the person reading the plan to see the financial implications over the full three-year planning period. The summary is presented as a simple diagram along the lines shown in Figure 12-3. The diagram is accompanied by a brief commentary. For example: "This three-year business plan shows an increase in revenue from 700 million to 900 million dollars, an increase in contribution from 100 thousand to 400 thousand dollars. The purpose of this marketing plan is to show how these increases will be achieved."

TABLE 12-1

	t–1	t–2	t–3	t–4	t–5	t–6
Sales						
Gross margin						
Research and development						
Selling, general and administrative						
Operating expenses						
Interest and other income (expense)						
Net Income						
Share of larger market						

t = time period (i.e., year or quarter)

203

Figure 12-3
Summary of
Financial
Projections

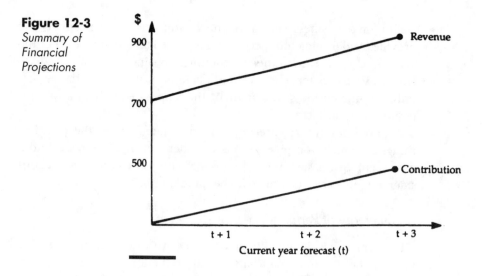

4. Market Overview

The market overview is intended to provide a brief picture of the market before getting to the particular details of individual market segments, which form the heart of the marketing plan. This system is based on the *segmentation* of markets. Markets are divided into groups of customers, each having characteristics that can be exploited in marketing terms. *This approach is taken because it is the most useful to enable managers to develop their markets.* The alternative, product-oriented approach is rarely appropriate, given the variation among customer groups in the markets in which most organizations compete.

Although it is difficult to give precise instructions on how to present this section of the marketing plan, it is possible (after completion of the marketing audit) to present a market overview that summarizes what managers consider to be the key characteristics of their markets. In completing this section, managers consider the following:

- What are the principal products, markets, or segments that are likely to provide the kinds of business opportunities suitable for the organization?
- How are these products, markets, or segments changing? That is, which are growing and which are declining?

This section is brief and contains commentary by management about what seems to be happening in their market. It is very helpful if managers can present as much of this information as possible visually (bar charts or pie charts, product life cycles). A market "map" can be extremely useful for clarifying how the market works (see chapter 3).

5. SWOT Analyses of Principal Products and Markets

Compiling the SWOT Analyses

To decide on marketing objectives and future strategy, it is first necessary to summarize your *present* position in the market. This is done in section 4. The marketing audit must now be summarized in the form of a number of *SWOT analyses* for the main products or markets (segments) highlighted in section 4. The acronym *SWOT* stands for *strengths, weaknesses, opportunities,* and *threats.* In simple terms, the analysis answers the following questions:

- What are the unit's differential strengths and weaknesses in relation to competitors? In other words, why should potential customers in the target markets prefer your offering over that of your competitors?
- What are the opportunities?
- What are the present and future threats to the business in each of the segments identified as being of importance?

Guidelines for Completing the SWOT Analysis

The market overview in section 4 identifies what you consider to be the key product or market (segments) on which you intend to focus. For presentation purposes, it is helpful if you can present a brief SWOT analysis for each of these key product or market segments. Each of these SWOT analyses should be brief and interesting to read. Complete SWOT analyses only for the key segments.

Section I of the analysis concerns strengths and weaknesses. Section II indicates how the opportunities and threats section of the SWOT is to be completed. Section III summarizes key issues to be addressed. Section IV describes the setting of assumptions, marketing objectives, and strategies for each product or market segment. Section V summarizes the position of competitors.

I. Important Factors for Success in This Business (Critical Success Factors)

How does a competitor that wants to provide products or services in this segment succeed? Relatively few factors determine success. Factors such as product performance, breadth of services, speed of service, and low costs are often the most important factors for success.

You should now make a brief statement about your organization's *strengths and weaknesses* in relation to the most important factors for success that you have identified. To do this, consider other suppliers to the same segment to identify why you believe your organization can succeed and what weaknesses must be addressed in the three-year planning period.

These factors are called critical success factors (CSFs). A layout such as that shown in Figure 12-4 is useful. Weight each factor on a scale of 100 (e.g., CSF 1 = 60; CSF 2 = 25; CSF 3 = 10; CSF 4 = 5). Score yourself and each competitor on a scale of ten on each of the CSFs. Multiply each score by the weight. This gives an accurate reading of your position in each segment in relation to your competitors. It also highlights which are the *key issues to address* in the three-year planning period.

Great caution is necessary to ensure that you are not guilty of self-delusion. It is desirable to have independent evidence from market research to complete this section accurately. If you do not have independent evidence, it is still worth conducting a SWOT analysis, because it at least indicates what you need to know. Also, it is valuable to get customers to complete this analysis. Frequently, this will reveal a great deal about what the customers believe to be the factors for success.

II. Summary of Outside Influences and Their Implications (Opportunities and Threats)

This summary includes a brief statement about how important environmental influences such as technology, government policies and regu-

Figure 12-4
Critical Success Factors

Competitors / Critical success factors	Weighting factor	Your organization	Competitor A	Competitor B	Competitor C
CSF 1					
CSF 2					
CSF 3					
CSF 4					
Total weighted score	100				

lations, and the economy have affected this segment. There always are obvious opportunities and threats.

III. Key Issues to Be Addressed

Sections I and II of the analysis will show a number of key issues to be addressed.

IV. Assumptions, Marketing Objectives, Marketing Strategies

Assumptions can now be made and objectives and strategies set. At this point assumptions, objectives, and strategies relate only to each particular product or market segment under consideration. These guide your thinking when setting overall assumptions, marketing objectives, and strategies later.

V. Competitor Analysis

Summarize the findings of the audit in respect to *major competitors* only. For each competitor, indicate the sales within the particular product or market segment under consideration, share now, *and expected share three years from now.* The greater a competitor's influence over others, the greater is its ability to implement its own independent strategies and the more successful they are. Also classify each of your main competitors according to one of the classifications in the guide to competitive position classifications, such as leadership, strong, favorable, tenable, or weak.

List competitors' principal products or services, and list each major competitor's business direction and current strategies. The format of Figure 12-5 provides a guideline to classifying business directions and business strategies. Next, list competitors' main strengths and weakness.

Guide to Competitive Position Classifications

Leadership	Has a major influence on the performance or behavior of others
Strong	Has a wide choice of strategies
	Is able to adopt an independent strategy without endangering short-term position
	Has low vulnerability to competitors' actions
Favorable	Exploits specific competitive strengths, often in a product-market niche
	Has more than average opportunity to improve position; has several strategies available
Tenable	Performance justifies continuation in business
Weak	Currently has an unsatisfactory performance and significant competitive weakness
	Must improve or withdraw

Figure 12-5

Competitor analysis					
Main competitor	Products/ markets	Business direction and current objectives and strategies	Strengths	Weaknesses	Competitive position

The following list includes five business directions that are appropriate for almost any business. Select those that best summarize the competitor's strategy.

Business Directions

Enter	To allocate resources to a new business area. Consideration includes building from prevailing company or division strengths, exploiting related opportunities, and defending against perceived threats.
Improve	To apply strategies that greatly improve the competitive position of the business. Often, this requires thoughtful product and market segmentation.
Maintain	To maintain one's competitive position. Aggressive strategies may be required, although a defensive posture may be assumed. Product and

	market position is maintained, often in a niche.
Harvest	To relinquish intentionally a competitive position, emphasizing short-term profit and cash flow, but not necessarily at the risk of losing the business in the short term. Often this requires consolidating or reducing various aspects of the business to gain higher performance for that which remains.
Exit	To divest a business because of its weak competitive position or because the cost of staying in business is prohibitive and the risk associated with improving position is too high.

6. Portfolio Summary (Summary of SWOTs)

All that remains is to summarize each of these SWOTs in a format that makes it easy to see at a glance the overall position and relative importance of each of these segments to the organization. This can be done by drawing a diagram in the form of a four-box *matrix* that shows each of the important product and market segments described earlier. A matrix is shown in Figure 12-6. Some easy-to-follow instructions follow on how to complete such a matrix. Detailed instructions are provided in chapter 4.

Figure 12-6
Portfolio Summary

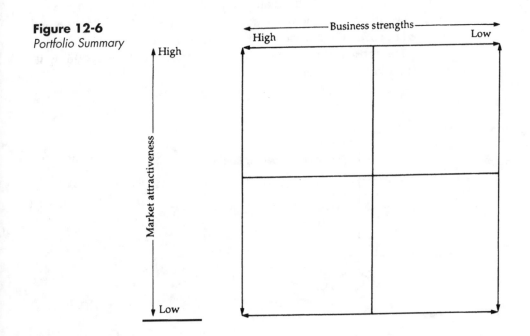

The *portfolio matrix* (called the *directional policy matrix* in chapter 4) enables you to assess which products or services, or which groups of customers and segments, will offer the best chance of market success. It also aids decision making about which products or services (or market segments) merit investment, in terms of both finance and managerial effort.

In this example, market segments are used, although it is possible to use products or services. We recommend that you use the following instructions to arrive at a portfolio matrix for your business:

1. List your market segments and decide which ones are the most attractive. (These segments can be countries, divisions, markets, distributors, customers.) To arrive at these decisions, you need to take many factors into account, including the following:

- The size and rate of growth of the markets
- Market needs
- Pricing conditions and trends
- The competition: quantity and quality
- The business environment
- Macrotrends and developments; technology, economic conditions, regulations

Imagine that you have a measuring instrument, something like a thermometer, that measures not temperature but market attractiveness. The higher the reading, the more attractive is the market. The instrument is shown in Figure 12-7. Estimate the position on the scale *each* of your markets would record and make a note of it. You should use the method outlined in chapter 4 and the example provided in Table 4-3.

2. Transpose this information on to the matrix in Figure 12-6, writing the markets on the left of the matrix.

Figure 12-7
Market
Attractiveness

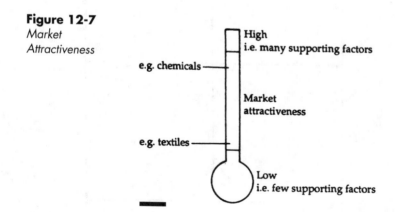

3. Still using the matrix, draw a dotted line horizontally across from the top left-hand market as shown in Figure 12-8.

4. Ask yourself how well your business is equipped to deal with this most attractive market. A series of questions has to be asked to establish the company's business strengths, for example:

- Do we have the right products?
- How well are we known in this market?
- What image do we have?
- Do we have the right technical skills?
- How close are we to this market?
- How do we compare with competitors?

The outcome of such an analysis enables you to arrive at a conclusion about the "fitness" of your unit, and you will be able to choose a point on the horizontal scale of the matrix to represent this. The left of the scale represents many unit strengths, the right few unit strengths. The SWOT analysis completed in section 5 is used, because you have already completed the necessary quantification. Draw a vertical line from this point on the scale as shown in Figure 12-9, so that it intersects with the horizontal line, and draw a circle at the point of intersection. (Be certain, however, to use the quantitative method outlined in chapter 4.)

5. *Redraw* the circles, this time making the diameter of each circle proportional to that segment's share of your total sales turnover. (To be technically correct you should take the square root of the volume, or value.)

6. Indicate where these circles will be in three years' time and their estimated size. The matrix may, therefore, have to show segments not currently served. There are two ways of showing this. First, in deciding on market or segment attractiveness you can assume that you are at t0 (i.e., today) and that your forecast of attractiveness covers the next three years (i.e., t + 3). If this is your chosen method, then it will be clear that *the circle*

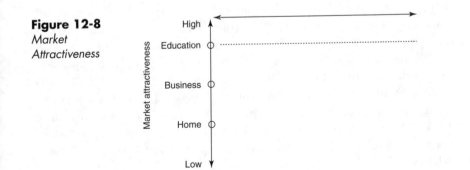

Figure 12-8
Market
Attractiveness

Figure 12-9
*Market Attractive-
ness and Business
Strengths*

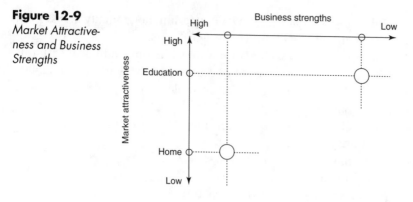

can only move horizontally along the axis, because all that changes is your business strength.

The second way to show segments not currently served shows the current attractiveness position on the vertical axis based on the past three years (i.e., t – 3 to t0) and then forecasts how that attractiveness position will change during the next three years (i.e., t0 to t + 3). In such a case, the circles can move both vertically and horizontally. This is the method used in the example provided (Figure 12-10), but it is entirely up to you which method you use. It is essential to be creative in your use of the matrix. Be prepared to change the name on the axes and to experiment with both products and markets.

7. Overall Assumptions

Each business must highlight the assumptions critical to the fulfillment of the planned marketing objectives and strategies. Key planning assumptions deal, in the main, with outside features and anticipated changes that would have substantial influence on the achievement of marketing objectives. These might include areas such as market growth rate, your organization's costs, and capital investment.

Assumptions should be few in number and relate only to key issues such as those identified in the SWOT analyses. If it is possible for a plan to be implemented irrespective of the assumptions made, those assumptions are not necessary and should be removed. You should find that the more detailed lists of assumptions made for each of the principal product or market segments analyzed in the SWOT stage (section 5) is helpful in deciding what the macro-assumptions should be.

Figure 12-10
Market Attractive-ness and Business Strengths

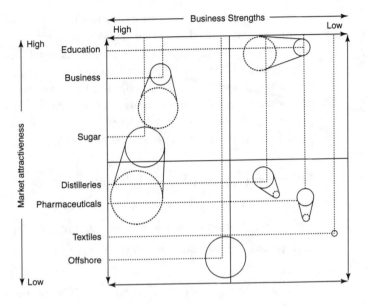

8. Overall Marketing Objectives and Strategies

Marketing Objectives

After you have identified and stated key strengths, weaknesses, opportunities, and threats and made an explicit statement of assumptions about conditions that affect the business, the process of setting marketing objectives is easy, because you have a realistic statement of what the business desires to achieve as a result of market-centered analysis.

As in the case of objective setting for other functional areas of the business, setting marketing objectives is the most important step in the process. It is a commitment on a business-wide basis to a particular course of action, which will determine the scheduling and costing out of subsequent actions.

An *objective* is what the unit wants to achieve. A *strategy* is how it plans to achieve it. There are objectives and strategies at all levels in marketing. For example, there can be advertising objectives and strategies and pricing objectives and strategies. However, the important point about marketing objectives is that they should be focused on creating a unique value for customers. Advertising, pricing, and other elements of the marketing mix are the means (the strategies) that define the unique value created by the firm. The market response to this offer determines the company's success.

Pricing objectives, sales promotion objectives, and advertising objectives are *not* to be confused with marketing objectives.

If profits and cash flows are to be maximized, it is important to consider carefully how current customer needs are changing and how products offered must change accordingly. Because change is inevitable, it is necessary to consider the two main dimensions of growth-product development and market development.

Marketing objectives are concerned with the following:

Selling existing products to existing segments

Developing new products for existing segments

Extending existing products to new segments

Developing new products for new segments

Marketing objectives are *quantitative*. They are expressed when possible in terms of *values, volumes,* and *market shares*. General directional terms such as "maximize," "minimize," and "penetrate" are avoided unless quantification is included. The marketing objectives cover the full three-year planning horizon and are accompanied by broad strategies (discussed in the following section) and broad revenue and cost projections for the full three-year period.

A key document in the annual planning round is the three-year strategic marketing plan. The one-year marketing plan should contain specific objectives for the first year of the three-year planning cycle and the corresponding strategies that will be used to achieve these objectives. *The one-year and the three-year plans are separate documents. At this stage, a detailed one-year plan is not required.*

Marketing Strategies

Marketing strategies state in broad terms *how* the marketing objectives are to be achieved, as follows:

The specific product policies (range, technical specifications, additions, deletions)

The pricing policies to be followed for product groups in particular market segments

The customer service levels to be provided for specific market segments (such as maintenance support)

The policies for communicating with customers under each of the main headings, such as sales force, advertising, sales promotion

Guidelines for setting marketing objectives and strategies are outlined in chapter 5. The following summarizes marketing objectives and strategy alternatives.

Objectives

Market penetration

Introduce new products to existing markets

Introduce existing products to new markets (domestic)

Introduce existing products to new markets (international)

Introduce new products to new markets

Strategies

Change product design, performance, quality, or features

Change advertising or promotion

Change unit price

Change delivery or distribution

Change service levels

Improve marketing productivity (e.g., improve the sales mix)

Improve administrative productivity

Consolidate product line

Withdraw from markets

Consolidate distribution

Standardize design

Acquire markets, products, facilities

Guidelines for Setting Marketing Objectives and Strategies

Completing a portfolio matrix for each major product or market segment with each unit translates the characteristics of the business into visible and easily understood positions in relation to each other. The position of each product or market segment on the matrix suggests broad goals that are usually appropriate for businesses in that position, although unit managers should also consider alternative goals in light of the special circumstances prevailing at the time. The four categories on the matrix are as follows:

Invest

Maintain position

Harvest cash

Selective investment

You may prefer to use your own terms, although it is not necessary to attach any particular name to any of the quadrants. Each category is considered in turn.

Invest

Products in the *invest* category enjoy competitive positions in markets or segments characterized by high growth rates and are good for continuing attractiveness. The objective for such products is to maintain growth rates at least at the market growth rate, maintaining market share and market leadership, or to grow faster than the market, increasing market share.

The following three principal factors should be considered:

Possible geographic expansion

Possible product line expansion

Possible product line differentiation

These can be achieved by means of internal development, acquisition, or joint ventures. The main point is that in attractive marketing situations such as this, *an aggressive marketing posture is required,* together with a tight budgeting and control process to ensure that capital resources are efficiently utilized.

Maintain Position

Products in the *maintain* category enjoy competitive positions in markets or segments not considered attractive in the long term. The thrust is toward maintaining a profitable position with greater emphasis on present earnings rather than on aggressive growth. The most successful product lines are maintained, and less successful ones are considered for pruning. Marketing effort is focused on differentiating products to maintain share of key segments of the market. Discretionary marketing expenditure is limited, especially when unchallenged by competitors or when products have matured. Comparative prices are stabilized, except when a temporary aggressive stance is necessary to maintain market share.

Harvest Cash

Products in the *profit* category have a poor position in unattractive markets. These products are "bad" only if objectives are not appropriate to the company's position in the market segment. In general, when immediate divestment is not warranted, these products are managed for cash. Product lines are aggressively pruned, and all marketing expenditure is minimized with prices maintained or, when possible, raised. A distinction must be made between different types of products. The two principal categories are as follows:

Those that are clearly uncompetitive in unattractive markets

Those that are near the dividing line

Products in the first category are managed as outlined earlier. The others are managed differently. For example, the reality of low growth is acknowledged, and the temptation is resisted to grow the product at its previous high rates of growth. Viewing low growth as a "marketing" problem would be likely to lead to high advertising, promotion, and inventory costs and lower profitability. Growth segments are identified and exploited when possible. Product quality is emphasized to avoid "commodity" competition. Productivity is systematically improved. Finally, the attention of talented managers is focused on these low-growth products.

Selective Investment

It is necessary to decide whether to invest for future market leadership in attractive markets or segments or to manage for present earnings. Both objectives are feasible, but managing these products for cash today is usually inconsistent with market share growth. It is usually necessary to select the most promising markets and invest in them only.

Additional Marketing and Other Functional Guidelines

We recommend that you consider three or more options before deciding on the best. Other marketing and functional guidelines to consider are outlined in chapter 5.

Database and Summary of Marketing Objectives

The summary is essential information that underpins the marketing plan. Included in the database are the following:

Market segment sales values that show, for a five-year period, total market demand, the sales in the business unit and the market share these represent for the various market segments

Market segment gross profits that show, for a five-year period, the business unit's sales value, gross profit, and gross margin for the various market segments

Product group analysis that shows, for a five-year period, the business unit's sales value, gross profit, and gross margin for different product groups

Summary (in words rather than numbers) of main marketing objectives and strategies

9. Financial Projections for Three Years

Provide financial projections, for the full three-year planning period under all the principal standard revenue and cost headings as specified by your organization.

Section B: The One-Year Marketing Plan

(This should be kept separate from the three-year strategic marketing plan and should not be completed until the planning team has approved the strategic plan in May each year.)

Specific sub-objectives for products and segments, supported by more detailed strategy and action statements, should now be developed. Here include *budgets* and *forecasts* and a *consolidated budget*. These must reflect the marketing objectives and strategies, and, in turn, the objectives, strategies, and programs *must* reflect the agreed-upon budgets and sales forecasts. Their main purposes are to delineate the major steps required in implementation, to assign accountability, to focus on the major decision points, and to specify the required allocation of resources and their timing.

If the procedures in this system are followed, a hierarchy of *objectives* will be built up in such a way that every item of budgeted expenditure can be related directly back to the initial financial objectives (this is known as *task-related budgeting*). Thus when, say, advertising has been identified as a means of achieving an objective in a particular market (i.e., advertising is a strategy to be used), all advertising expenditure against items appearing in the budget can be related back specifically to a major objective. The essential feature of this is that budgets are set against both the overall marketing objectives and the sub-objectives for each element of the marketing mix.

The principal advantage is that this method allows operating units to build up and demonstrate an increasingly clear picture of their markets. This method of budgeting also allows every item of expenditure to be fully accounted for as part of an objective approach. It also ensure that when changes have to be made during the period to which the plan relates, such changes can be made in a way that causes the least damage to the SBU's long-term objectives.

Note that it is important to include a *contingency plan* in the one-year marketing plan, as discussed below.

Guidelines for Completion of a One-Year Marketing Plan

Because of the varying nature of companies and industries, it is impossible to provide a standard format for all companies. There is, however, a minimum amount of information that should be provided to accompany the financial documentation between September and October. There is no need to supply market background information, as this should have been completed in the three-year strategic marketing plan.

Suggested Format for a One-Year Marketing Plan

1. (a) *Overall objectives*—should cover the following:
   - Volume or value share of target market
     - Previous five years
     - Current year estimate
     - Plan: next year
   - Gross margin
     - Previous five years
     - Current year estimate
     - Plan: next year

   Along with each there should be a few words of commentary/explanation.

   (b) *Overall strategies*—e.g., new customers, new products, advertising, sales promotion, selling, customer service, pricing. For a list of marketing strategies, see chapter 5.

2. (a) *Sub-objectives*—more detailed objectives should be provided for products, or markets, or segments, or major customers, as appropriate.

   (b) *Strategies*—the means by which sub-objectives will be achieved should be stated.

(c) *Action/tactics*—the details, timing, responsibility, and cost should also be stated.

3. *Summary of marketing activities and costs.*

4. *Contingency plan*—it is important to include a contingency plan, which should address the following questions:

(a) What are the critical assumptions on which the one-year plan is based?

(b) What would the financial consequences be (i.e., the effect on the operating income) if these assumptions did not come true? For example, if a forecast of revenue is based on the assumption that a major customer will build a new plant, what would the effect be if that customer did not go ahead?

(c) How will these assumptions be measured?

(d) What action will you take to ensure that the adverse financial effects of an unfulfilled assumption are mitigated, so that you end up with the same forecast profit at the end of the year?

To measure the risk, assess the negative or downside, asking what can go wrong with each assumption that would change the outcome. For example, if a market growth rate of 5 percent is a key assumption, what lower growth rate would have to occur before a substantially different management decision would be taken? For a capital project, this would be the point at which the project would cease to be economical.

5. *Operating result and financial ratios*—this should include:
   - Net revenue
   - Gross margin
   - Adjustments
   - Marketing costs
   - Administration costs
   - Interest
   - Operating result
   - ROS (return on sales)
   - ROI (return on investment)

6. *Key activity planner*—finally, you should summarize the key activities and indicate the start and finish. This should help you considerably with monitoring the progress of your annual plan.

7. *Other*—there may be other information you wish to provide, such as sales call plans.

Authors' Note

EXMAR©, PowerStrat©, and StratPlan© are decision-support tools for strategic marketing planning based on the process outlined in this book. Professor Malcolm McDonald of the Cranfield School of Management in the UK and Professor Warren J. Keegan of Pace University in New York and Visiting Professor at ESSEC (France) are world authorities on marketing strategy. Their expertise has guided the development of this software.

BENEFITS OF DECISION-SUPPORT SOFTWARE

- Allows you to explore "what-if?" scenarios
- Saves time in formulating strategy so that you have more time to implement and refine your strategy
- Identifies the data you need to formulate strategy and provides a data-capture framework
- Automatically organizes this data to create information that will assist you to:
  - identify strategy alternatives
  - sharpen your customer focus
  - create greater value for your target customers
  - speed up your reaction/response time to market and competitive behavior changes
  - increase your market share and profitability

DECISION-SUPPORT SOFTWARE

EXMAR©, PowerStrat©, and StratPlan© are complete, robust packages with supporting services. They are not "off the shelf" template software in a shrink-wrapped package with a manual. Each package includes custom-tailored consulting assistance to ensure that you and your organization are able to fully implement the marketing planning processes described in this book.

Strategic Marketing Planning Process

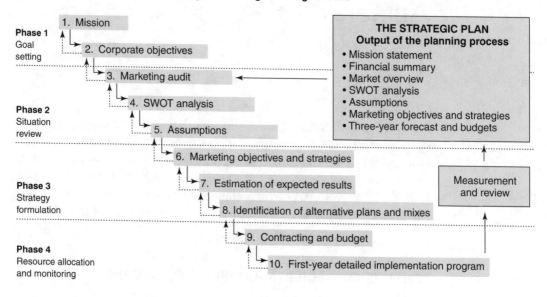

There are a number of techniques, methodologies, concepts, and frameworks integrated in these packages, including:

- Gap analysis
- SWOT analysis
- Ansoff Matrix
- Value Curve Analysis
- Directional Policy Matrix (DPM)
- Porter's Five Forces
- Porter's Strategic Positions

These tools facilitate the creation of strategies that take account of differences in product or service requirements in different market segments. They assist companies by:

- Guiding them through a logical marketing planning process
- Defining the key data requirements
- Displaying information graphically to aid understanding of the business
- Allowing "what if?" analyses
- Automatically generating reports and presentations from the analysis

For more information about how you can take advantage of these tools to speed up and sharpen your strategic marketing planning, contact:

The Competitive Strategy Group
210 Stuyvesant Avenue
Rye, NY 10580
Telephone: 914-967-9421
Fax: 914-967-2991
e-mail: keegan@pace.edu

Index

Butterworth-Heinemann Business Books . . .
for Transforming Business

5th Generation Management: Co-creating Through Virtual Enterprising, Dynamic Teaming, and Knowledge Networking, Revised Edition,
   Charles M. Savage, 0-7506-9701-6

After Atlantis: Working, Managing, and Leading in Turbulent Times,
   Ned Hamson, 0-7506-9884-5

The Alchemy of Fear in the Workplace
   Kay Gilley, 0-7506-9909-4

Beyond Strategic Vision: Effective Corporate Action with Hoshin Planning,
   Michael Cowley and Ellen Domb, 0-7506-9843-8

Beyond Time Management: Business with Purpose,
   Robert A. Wright, 0-7506-9799-7

The Breakdown of Hierarchy: Communicating in the Evolving Workplace,
   Eugene Marlow and Patricia O'Connor Wilson, 0-7056-9746-6

Business and the Feminine Principle: The Untapped Resource,
   Carol R. Frenier, 0-7506-9829-2

Choosing the Future: The Power of Strategic Thinking,
   Stuart Wells, 0-7506-9876-4

Cultivating Common Ground: Releasing the Power of Relationships at Work,
   Daniel S. Hanson, 0-7506-9832-2

Flight of the Phoenix: Soaring to Success in the 21st Century,
   John Whiteside and Sandra Egli, 0-7506-9798-9

Getting a Grip on Tomorrow: Your Guide to Survival and Success in the Changed World of Work,
   Mike Johnson, 0-7506-9758-X

Innovation Strategy for the Knowledge Economy: The Ken *Awakening,*
   Debra M. Amidon, 0-7506-9841-1

The Intelligence Advantage: Organizing for Complexity,
   Michael D. McMaster, 0-7506-9792-X

Intuitive Imagery: A Resource at Work,
   John B. Pehrson and Susan E. Mehrtens, 0-7506-9805-5

The Knowledge Evolution: Expanding Organizational Intelligence,
   Verna Allee, 0-7506-9842-X

Leadership in a Challenging World: A Sacred Journey,
   Barbara Shipka, 0-7506-9750-4

Leading from the Heart: Choosing Courage over Fear in the Workplace,
   Kay Gilley, 0-7506-9835-7

Learning to Read the Signs: Reclaiming Pragmatism in Business,
   F. Byron Nahser, 0-7506-9901-9

Leveraging People and Profit: The Hard Work of Soft Management,
   Bernard A. Nagle and Perry Pascarella, 0-7506-9961-2

A Place to Shine: Emerging from the Shadows at Work,
   Daniel S. Hanson, 0-7506-9738-5

Power Partnering: A Strategy for Business Excellence in the 21st Century,
   Sean Gadman, 0-7506-9809-8

Putting Emotional Intelligence to Work: Successful Leadership is More Than IQ,
   David Ryback, 0-7506-9956-6

Resources for the Knowledge-Based Economy Series

   The Knowledge Economy,
      Dale Neef, 0-7506-9936-1

   Knowledge Management and Organizational Design,
      Paul S. Myers, 0-7506-9749-0

   Knowledge Management Tools,
      Rudy L. Ruggles, III, 0-7506-9849-7

   Knowledge in Organizations,
      Laurence Prusak, 0-7506-9718-0

   The Strategic Management of Intellectual Capital,
      David A. Klein, 0-7506-9850-0

Setting the PACE® in Product Development: A Guide to Product And Cycle-time Excellence,
   Michael E. McGrath, 0-7506-9789-X

Time to Take Control: The Impact of Change on Corporate Computer Systems,
   Tony Johnson, 0-7506-9863-2

The Transformation of Management,
   Mike Davidson, 0-7506-9814-4

What is the Emperor Wearing? Truth-Telling in Business Relationships,
   Laurie Weiss, 0-7506-9872-1

Who We Could Be at Work, Revised Edition,
   Margaret A. Lulic, 0-7506-9739-3

Working From Your Core: Personal and Corporate Wisdom in a World of Change,
   Sharon Seivert, 0-7506-9931-0

**To purchase any Butterworth-Heinemann title,
please visit your local bookstore or call 1-800-366-2665.**